A Scent (

MW00795419

A Scent of Sandalwood

Indo-Ismaili Religious Lyrics (Ginans)
Volume 1

❧

SELECTED AND TRANSLATED, WITH AN
INTRODUCTION, INTERPRETATIVE ESSAY
AND NOTES

Aziz Esmail

CURZON

First Published in 2002
by Curzon Press
Richmond, Surrey
http://www.curzonpress.co.uk

in association with The Institute of Ismaili Studies
42–44 Grosvenor Gardens, London SW1W 0EB
website: http://www.iis.ac.uk

Typeset in New Baskerville by LaserScript Ltd, Mitcham, Surrey
Printed and bound in Great Britain by
Biddles Ltd, Guildford and King's Lynn

British Library Cataloguing in Publication Data
A catalogue record of this book is available from the British Library

Library of Congress Cataloguing in Publication Data
A catalogue record for this book has been requested

ISBN 0–7007–1767–6 (hbk)
ISBN 0–7007–1768–4 (pbk)

The Institute of Ismaili Studies

The Institute of Ismaili Studies was established in 1977 with the object of promoting scholarship and learning on Islam, in the historical as well as contemporary contexts, and a better understanding of its relationship with other societies and faiths.

The Institute's programmes encourage a perspective which is not confined to the theological and religious heritage of Islam, but seeks to explore the relationship of religious ideas to broader dimensions of society and culture. The programmes thus encourage an interdisciplinary approach to the materials of Islamic history and thought. Particular attention is also given to issues of modernity that arise as Muslims seek to relate their heritage to the contemporary situation.

Within the Islamic tradition, the Institute's programmes seek to promote research on those areas which have, to date, received relatively little attention from scholars. These include the intellectual and literary expressions of Shi'ism in general, and Ismailism in particular.

In the context of Islamic societies, the Institute's programmes are informed by the full range and diversity of cultures in which Islam is practised today, from the Middle East, South and Central Asia, and Africa to the industrialised societies of the West, thus taking into consideration the variety of contexts which shape the ideals, beliefs and practices of the faith.

These objectives are realised through concrete programmes and activities organised and implemented by various departments of the Institute. The Institute also collaborates periodically, on a programme-specific basis, with other institutions of learning in the United Kingdom and abroad.

The Institute's academic publications fall into several distinct and interrelated categories:

1 Occasional papers or essays addressing broad themes of the relationship between religion and society in the historical as well as modern contexts, with special reference to Islam.
2 Monographs exploring specific aspects of Islamic faith and culture, or the contributions of individual Muslim figures or writers.
3 Editions or translations of significant primary or secondary texts.
4 Translations of poetic or literary texts which illustrate the rich heritage of spiritual, devotional and symbolic expressions in Muslim history.
5 Works on Ismaili history and thought, and the relationship of the Ismailis to other traditions, communities and schools of thought in Islam.
6 Proceedings of conferences and seminars sponsored by the Institute.
7 Bibliographical works and catalogues which document manuscripts, printed texts and other source materials.

This book falls into category four listed above.

In facilitating these and other publications, the Institute's sole aim is to encourage original research and analysis of relevant issues. While every effort is made to ensure that the publications are of a high academic standard, there is naturally bound to be a diversity of views, ideas and interpretations. As such, the opinions expressed in these publications must be understood as belonging to their authors alone.

Contents

Preface and Acknowledgements

As I say in the Introduction, these translations from the corpus of religious poetry known as the Ginans have a twofold inspiration: a long familiarity dating back to childhood, which ensured their poetic, emotional and musical appeal; and an enduring interest in the English language and its literature. The genesis of these translations, however, was purely circumstantial. While at the Committee on Social Thought at the University of Chicago, I had occasion to observe and appreciate the work of the late A. K. Ramanujan, distinguished by his equally perceptive feel for the pulse of English as well as South Indian poetry, and for the art of literature as well as the scientific discipline of linguistics. Conversations with him led to my trying a translation of a few verses from the Ginans. Ramanujan's pleasure at these was encouraging, as was also, similarly, the positive comments of Wendy Doniger O'Flaherty. And so the ambition to extend the attempt took root.

Several years later, thanks to the interest of its then Director, Professor John Carman, the Centre for the Study of Religion at Harvard University sponsored my stay there to enable the project to be completed. Professor Carman's enthusiasm for the translations was a great boost to the project. And although the work was later laid aside for various reasons, I was fortunate to find that the translations stayed in Professor Carman's memory. Whenever our paths crossed during succeeding years, he never failed to press me, with his characteristic gentleness and warmth, to let the work see the light of day. It is with great pleasure that this memory has returned to my mind as the work begun in his presence now approaches fruition, so that I can at last thank him, through this book, for the kindness and support which provided the crucial, initial impetus to the work. Needless to say, in whatever respects these translations fall short of the best standards of the enterprise (and there are bound to be many), responsibility for them is entirely mine.

Nearer in time, a number of colleagues and friends have provided valuable moral support, of whom I would like to mention, in particular, Professor Azim Nanji (who has long shared my appreciation for this literature); my colleagues on the Board of Governors of the Institute; Dr. Karim Janmohamed; and Iqbal Rupani (himself a discerning judge of literatures in both these languages). The interest and goodwill of these and other individuals contributed more to the successful completion of this work than they probably realise. For few writers can dispense with the benevolent presence, in their minds, of a potential reader-ship, whose anticipation of the work serves as a beacon, encouraging perseverance at one's chosen task in spite of the frustrations and doubts which beset most writers, in the midst of their labours, from time to time.

A number of other individuals have been of direct, dedicated assistance in the completion of this work. I am indebted, first of all, to Alnoor Merchant, who, out of his kindness and personal regard, as well as a genuine affection for the subject, put in long hours, despite other pressing calls on his time, to assist in the final, technical stages of this work.

Kutub Kassam helped the work through, in the final stage, by applying his meticulous regard for the conventions of language, his feel for poetry, and his fine appreciation of the subject, to the text of the work. My thanks are due to him for the sustained effort he put in, and the suggestions he made for the improvement, in several places, of the penultimate text.

The language and terminology of the Ginans presents many obstacles to a modern reader or translator. Conventional tools, such as dictionaries, are of no help when the terminology bears the stamp of oral, regional and historical idiosyncrasies. The work has benefited, in this context, from the contribution of Shafique Virani, currently at Harvard. I am grateful for the promptness and goodwill with which he put his scholarly knowledge of the terminology in the Ginans at my disposal, whenever I had occasion to ask him for his understanding of specific terms and allusions in the texts.

Lastly, this book owes its existence in the present form to Miss Rita Bishopp, my Personal Assistant, who not only word-processed my original manuscript, but constantly updated it by incorporating the numerous and seemingly incessant revisions to which I kept subjecting it. She handled these with characteristic cheerfulness and dedication, far surpassing the call of duty, for which I am most grateful to her.

I am tempted to offer here a suggestion to the type of general reader who may be interested in the poetry but liable to be deterred by the philosophical analysis in the Introduction. Lest it keep him (or her) from going on to enjoy the poetry, I would like to assure him that the core of the book lies in the voice of the poetry, and that it is not necessary for the analytic essays to be read before reading the translations. To such readers, I would suggest the following order of perusal. They should start with individual Ginans, followed by the notes on each, which are intended to draw attention to the structural and linguistic features of each piece. It cannot be stressed too strongly that the notes to each Ginan are consulted after, rather than before, reading the piece in question, so as not to prejudice the spontaneous appreciation of the poetry, and to allow full freedom for testing any commentary against the reader's own fresh impressions. The same principle may be applied to the overall comment in the Interpretative Essay. The Introduction may be left to the last (for this type of reader), though if he is curious about the principles which have guided my translations, he may wish to glance at section VIII of this essay at some stage in the process.

Introduction

I

The literary critic, George Steiner, has said of literary criticism – the intellectual appreciation of literature – that it must arise 'out of a debt of love'. The same must be said of translation.

Through these translations of the Ginans, I have tried to fulfil, however imperfectly, a double debt of love: on one hand, to medieval Indian literature (of which this poetry is a part) and the view of life reflected in it; and on the other hand, to the riches of the English language and literature and the vision of the world (in common with European literature) it represents.

Every translation is a traffic between worlds apart in space and time. The Latin origins of 'translate' take us, via the kindred 'transfer', to *trans – ferre*, 'to bear or carry across'. In essence, translation is a transportation from one mental or spiritual space to another. Or we might say, to use the term favoured by A. K. Ramanujan, that it is a 'translocation'. This last term has the merit of reminding us that an object re-located in space acquires a different look and meaning. We see this all the time in museums, art exhibits and household design. Verbal environment operates on verbal units in a way very similar to that in which physical environment acts on physical objects. Even where a word in one language is the exact equivalent of a word in another – not a circumstance to be commonly encountered – the new syntax in which it comes to be placed contributes new nuances of meaning. The process extends beyond language. It lies at the heart of the encounter of human cultures. Seen in this light, translation is but a case of human culture carried across in time and space.

Translating the Ginans highlights a twofold fact. In common with all poetic translations, it poses the challenge of negotiating between two languages, each with its specific genius and limitations. But it also makes one aware that the poetry itself was a translation, an act of commerce between not only different languages, but different cultural and religious traditions. By common consent, the Ginans were the outcome of a process of religious conversion. But we must remember that 'conversion' is a deceptively simple concept; and religious conversion is a still more complicated idea. In our day, when religious identities have sharply etched boundaries reflecting the modern state-system, with its constitutional demarcations between an 'inside' and an 'outside', conversion marks a conscious repudiation of one over-arching identity in favour of another. But in earlier history things were not quite the same. We need to bear this difference in mind, lest we miss the real complexion of this literature.

I shall return to this issue further below. First, however, we need to note the basic facts about the Ginans.

II

The Ginans are hymns, religious lyrics, which have for long been a central part of the religious life of the Indian Nizari Ismaili community (known as Khojas), and of which they continue to form the living religious tradition. The literature is also shared by the Imamshahi community in Gujarat, who are believed to have split off from the Ismailis sometime in the 16th century.[1] The Imamshahis call themselves 'Satpanthis'. But the term 'Satpanth', occurring in the Ginans, pre-dates the Imamshahi split. Literally meaning 'the true path', it is the name used in the Ginans for the faith preached in them. We shall here employ the term in this original, generic sense.

The term 'Ginan' is believed to derive from the Sanskrit *jnān*, an abstract noun, which may be variously rendered as 'knowledge', 'wisdom' or 'cognition' (reminiscent, to some extent, of the Greek *gnosis*). In the Indian Ismaili tradition it has come to refer to the individual hymns, and is thus treated as a countable name. It is in this sense that the term will be used in the present work (with the English plural ending 's' being added as necessary), apart from occasional use also as a collective noun: e.g. 'Ginan-literature'.

The Ginans are a vast corpus consisting of several hundred (indeed, by some estimates over a thousand) hymns. Some are short, the shortest consisting of as few as four verses. The longest run into several hundred verses. Unlike the shorter ones, the long compositions have titles, sometimes alluding to the content, and sometimes indicating the form (e.g. *saloko,* from the Sanskrit *sloka,* a metrical unit). Few Ginans, if any, can be distinguished by content. What rather gives each its unity, its identity, is the melody (*rāga*) assigned to it. Furthermore, the last verse of every Ginan mentions, without fail, the name of its accepted author. It is these features which make every single composition, whose content is normally quite heterogeneous, recognisably distinct.

The language of the Ginans is fascinatingly mixed. Its vocabulary is derived alike from Sanskrit, and languages descended from Sanskrit (chiefly Gujarati) on one hand, and Arabic and Persian on the other (though the syntax – grammar – is of Indian languages, mainly Gujarati, and not of Arabic or Persian). Similarly, Arabo-Persian vocabulary occurs with phonetic and grammatical adaptations to Indian diction (mainly Gujarati). The other Indian languages which feature besides Gujarati include Khari Boli (precursor to modern Hindi and Urdu), Punjabi, Sindhi and Siraiki (or Multani). Among these, Gujarati predominates.

Indian Ismaili tradition attributes the origin of this poetry to several charismatic figures or Pirs. The identity of the Pirs is one of the points on which critical scholarship and religious tradition appear to be in conflict. The last fifty years has seen the appearance of a series of scholarly studies on this subject.[2] The majority of them have been sceptical of the factual reliability of the accounts in the tradition of the dates and identities of the Pirs. Some go further, and either propose a later origin of the Ginans than is commonly believed or else, assuming the hypothesis of earlier origin, propose the likelihood of changes and interpolations during the period of their transmission in time and place. By contrast, tradition has never been in doubt about the identity of the Pirs, and their composition of the Ginans.

Not surprisingly, therefore, the conclusions of such scholarship have met with opposition from some, among the adherents of the tradition, who hold it dear and find in this literature the meaning and inspiration of their lives, and therefore regard this critical treatment of the tradition to be a gratuitous debunking. This controversy is one manifestation of a much broader phenomen-

3

on. Anyone aware of modern history will recognise in it a characteristic tension between religious belief and modern critical scholarship. It is an issue too important to ignore. The principles at stake in each case – critical inquiry on one hand, commitment to tradition on the other – are of deep human value and significance. Unfortunately, the academic tradition (and the tradition of historical scholarship in particular) is as prone to narrowness (in a sense I shall indicate later) as are traditions of belief. Happily, however, if the issue can ill-afford a stand-off, neither does it necessitate it. It can only be resolved, though, if both positions, rather than contending as rivals, subject themselves to a third, arbitrating point of view.

The present work aims at a literary translation and appreciation of the Ginans. My interest does not lie in a reconstruction of its history – its origins, the pathways of its transmission, and the state of the extant manuscripts. (I should add, though, that the contents of such manuscripts as I have consulted for purposes of this translation, are remarkably similar, if not uniform. This fact should serve to suggest a degree of care and scrupulousness in the preservation of the tradition). The religious power of the poetry and its lyrical beauty are such as to deserve study in its own right, irrespective of these historical issues. This is what the present work is intended to do.

It follows that I have no factual or scholarly detail to offer, by way of addition or amendment, to the historical observations and speculations made by scholars working in the field. This does not mean, however, that no *philosophical* critique is possible or necessary. I shall attempt this further below. For the present, I should simply like to summarise the facts about the Pirs and their lives as they are given in the tradition. In doing so, I bear the observations of scholarship in mind insofar as they are pertinent, though I will not discuss them here. This section is not, thus, my original contribution: I offer it only by way of a condensed introduction to a new reader, unacquainted alike with the tradition and the scholarship.

III

In noting reports in the tradition of the Pirs, especially the early figures, one is struck by the superhuman qualities attributed to them, not least in the impressive miracles they are said to have performed. Three points may be said about this at the outset. These accounts are best seen not as legendary in the negative sense, i.e., as 'unrealistic', but in the positive sense, rather, as having a mythopoetic reality. I shall have occasion later to return to this characteristic aspect of religious imagination.

Secondly, it is important to recognise that these reports are hardly atypical. They are quite standard in accounts of saints, ancestral figures and mystical preachers in all religious traditions where charismatic leadership (a concept which should be understood in not only religious but also sociological terms) functions as a counterpoint to orthodox, routinised or (to use the term favoured by the anthropologist, Clifford Geertz) 'scripturalist' religion.

Thirdly, in popular religiosity in the Indian Subcontinent, it is striking how the miracles attributed to different heroic figures in different religious traditions or communities are similar, if not identical. This fact has implications for the nature of religious identities in this historical milieu, to be discussed further below.

The earliest Pir to have preached in India, according to the Khoja Ismaili tradition, is one named Satgur Nur (or Nur Satgur). Various dates have been proposed for his life, falling in the period between the end of the 11th and the beginning of the 12th centuries. He is said to have won the allegiance of a Rajput king, Siddharaja Jayasinha, after a series of miracles, during which he made idols of Hindu deities dance and fetch water at his command. From there he proceeded to Navsara where, in what maybe described as a scene of true pastoral drama, he is said to have won the hand of the local princess in marriage. Traditions in the community trace the ancestry of Satgur Nur to the Shia Imam Ja'far al-Sadiq (died 765). As all the succeeding major Pirs (to be discussed below) are held in the tradition to be lineally descended from one another, this attributes Alid descent (i.e., from 'Ali b. Abu Talib, the first Shia Imam) to all these Pirs. It is worth noting, in this connection, that it was a common practice among the Sufis, more widely, for the descent of their Pirs to be traced back to the reputed figure of Ja'far al-Sadiq.[3]

Much greater feats (including making the sun descend to earth) have been attributed to Pir Shams, the second major figure in the tradition. Again, various dates have been proposed for him, the earlier ones depicting him as active in the first part of the 12th century, while others place him in the 14th century. One of his main theatres of activity was Multan, where he is credited with a number of impressive miracles. These include an almost comic battle of wills between him and the well-known Sufi, Bahauddin Zakariya. The story goes as follows. Fearing Pir Shams' arrival, Bahauddin orders boats in the river to be withdrawn. Pir Shams sets sail, therefore, in a paper ship. Along the way, the ship starts wavering, causing Pir Shams to wonder whether one of his companions is carrying worldly goods. Discovering one of them to be carrying jewels, he orders the jewellery to be thrown overboard. The ship continues on its smooth course, only to be stopped, however, by Pir Bahauddin's hostile stare from the window of his palace. Pir Shams returns the stare, and instantly a pair of horns sprout on Bahauddin's head, locking it outside the window. The boat continues on its course at full speed, and Pir Shams arrives in the town. No sooner than he has reached the local mosque, two sons of the panic-stricken Pir Bahauddin arrive in breathless haste to acknowledge Pir Shams' superior status, and beg for their father's release. Pir Shams duly relents, but legend has it that Bahauddin and his progeny were for ever to display the relics of the horns on their heads.[4]

There has been endless speculation about Pir Shams' identity (as the various dates cited above should show). The figures with whom he is identified include Shams-i Tabriz, the object of adoration of the famous Persian poet, Jalal al-Din Rumi. Such identifications, however, are historically shaky, and the community's tradition itself takes the view of him as an independent figure.

Pir Shams' Ginans include a number which are in Punjabi. A community of his followers in Punjab called *Shamsis*, hitherto practising their faith in secret, came out as Ismailis only in the last century. Elsewhere, a cycle of Ginans called *Garbis*, lyrics set to dance, commemorates Pir Shams' conversion of Hindu villagers at Analvaḍ, apparently in Gujarat, where he is said to have joined in their dance during the festival of *navrātri*, and substituted his own words for theirs, thus weaning them of their beliefs. Like many narratives of conversion, this story is commemorative, and may well reflect the tendency to condense into a single, concentrated episode, events which might have occurred over a long period and possibly also in different places. Bahauddin Zakariya apparently features in comparable legendary tales among other groups in the region[5] – a fact which serves to link this and other stories about Pir Shams to a common pool of such traditions.

The next notable name is that of Pir Sadardin. He is a figure of great stature, reported to have died anytime between the latter decades of the 14th century and the early decades of the 15th. His work is said to have spanned Sind, Punjab, Kutch and Kathiawad. Pir Sadardin is regarded by Khoja Ismailis as their founder as a community. The very name 'Khoja', said to be a corruption of the Persian *Khwajah* (in spirit equivalent to our 'gentleman') is believed to have been given by him. Similarly, he is credited with the setting up of the first *jamātkhānā* (communal centre) at Koṭḍi (in Sind) and appointing its religious head, the *mukhi* (very likely from *mukhya*, meaning 'chief'). He is also said to have given the congregation its vernacular prayer (*duā*). It is significant to note, however, that so far as I can ascertain, his own Ginans do not themselves refer to any of these events.[6]

The Ginans of the next major figure, Pir Hasan Kabirdin, a son of Pir Sadardin, are especially remarkable for their plaintive, ardent quality. Living in the 15th century, he spent most of his life in the town of Ucch, to the south of Multan. The tradition describes him as a man with a serious, forbearing outlook, and great strength of character. This makes him the first figure in the tradition to be sketched with a degree of personal (as opposed to archetypal or mythical) detail. Also interesting are reports of his reputation as a holy man not just among his own followers, but among other local communities (especially Sufis) as well. Thus, the Suhrawardi order reckoned him as one of their own Pirs.

There is a touching story of how Hasan Kabirdin, when still a young boy, was keen to accompany his father on one of his pilgrimages to Iran to visit the Ismaili Imam, Islamshah. As may be expected, the overland journey at the time was extremely arduous and dangerous. Quite sensibly, Pir Sadardin refused, putting down his son's importunities to a youthful excess of enthusiasm. Heartbroken, the young boy decided to compose, in a true labour of love, a poetic petition on an epic scale, to the Imam. The story relates how, extracting fibre from the fruit of a wild cotton plant, spinning it into yarn, and weaving a fabric, the young devotee made it into a turban into which he inscribed, strand by strand, his heartfelt words of yearning. Meanwhile Pir Sadardin, reaching the headquarters of the Imam in Iran, found his passage inexplicably blocked by a 'wall of iron'. For six months and six days, it is said, he held vigil at the gates, awaiting entry, while his little son completed his labours. Thus admonished, Pir Sadardin relented and sent word for his son to be fetched. The story describes how Hasan Kabirdin, crossing the huge land-mass to Iran, and arriving at Islamshah's court, presented him with the turban, the testimony to his soul. Greatly touched, the Imam put it on, and designated Hasan Kabirdin to succeed his father as Pir.[7]

Pir Hasan Kabirdin's death seems to have touched off events culminating in the first major schism in the Khoja community. The youngest of his eighteen sons, Imamshah, who was away at the time, is said to have hurried home but, meeting the funeral on its way, found himself cheated by his brothers of what he believed to be his rightful inheritance. During the succeeding row, which halted the funeral proceedings, the deceased father is said to have indicated his blessings to Imamshah by extending his hand from the bier and presenting him with a rosary and a lump of sugar.

Soon afterwards, Imamshah proceeded to Iran where, after meeting the Imam, according to one of his own mythical compositions, he was granted a visit to paradise. There he had a meeting, among others, with his deceased grandfather, Pir Sadardin. However, succession to his father appears to have eluded him, as the Imam is reported to have preferred a brother of the late Pir, by the name of Tajdin, to succeed him. Upon his return, however, Pir Tajdin met with opposition from some of his followers, who accused him of wrongful appropriation of goods not meant for him. He is also said, furthermore, to have been physically assaulted and beaten. These indictments and attacks seem to have led to his untimely death, while still a youth, through injury, shock or suicide.[8]

These events are related in a Ginan attributed to Nurmohamed Shah, a son of Imamshah, in terms which clearly indicate an intense struggle for power and position among Imamshah's sons and their followers. Vladimir Ivanow, who was the first Orientalist to write about the Imamshahi sect, was of the opinion that Imamshah was not himself responsible for the schism, which he attributed to Nurmohamed Shah. Similarly, tradition within the Indian Ismailis largely absolves Imamshah (and for that matter, his son too) from responsibility for the schism, though it concedes the possibility that Imamshah might have allowed himself to stray from his earlier loyalties. It adds that either this late defection, or very likely the activities of his later descendants, was responsible for the split. At any rate, Imamshah's Ginans were part of the corpus published earlier in the last century by the Ismaili community in Bombay.[9]

Whatever the facts about the specific personalities involved, the events following Imamshah's death mark a turning point in the history of the Ginanic tradition and its followers. In part, they suggest a renewed capacity and desire, at the headquarters of the Imam resident in Iran, to exert greater control over the community in the Subcontinent. In part, they exhibit an assertion of local autonomy – a natural instinct in human societies under external or overarching control, against the forces of centralisation. In part, they reveal proclivities of self-aggrandisement, dissension and intrigue among the descendants of Imamshah, who do not appear to have inherited the gifts and the stature of the great Pirs or indeed of Imamshah himself (who seems to have had a powerful, charismatic personality). Lastly, they suggest fluid, overlapping identities in the period in question. It is easy to see that the Ginanic motifs, being often symbolic rather than historically concrete, could well be claimed and drawn upon by groups with different allegiances. And this is indeed what seems to have occurred through succeeding years.

A more subtle form of evidence for these suppositions is to be found in a distinguishing feature of Nurmohamed's Ginans, setting them apart from the compositions of his predecessors. The latter are predominantly mythical, and such characters as appear in them are archetypal. Indeed, the Pirs to whom the Ginans are attributed are themselves archetypal, larger-than-life figures. Pir Shams, with the legendary feats and roles ascribed to him, falls obviously in this category. So does Pir Sadardin, who is placed in the Indian mythical scheme of salvation, erected on a cosmic scale. Pir Hasan Kabirdin follows him in this role. With Imamshah, we have legend partly penetrated by history. Nurmohamed Shah's Ginans are atypical in including stories, themselves largely legendary, of figures who also belong to history. The names of his successors, the Saiyads, come to us with information, however rudimentary, of their personalities. All in all, it would appear that a dim light of terrestrial history begins to shine on part of the ground previously given over to great cosmic myths and dramatisations.

Two interconnected trends characterise the period from now on. Attempts at consolidation of control from the headquarters of the Imam is one of these. Periodic breakaways and the emergence of dissident groups within the following in the Subcontinent is the other unmistakable feature. Effective consolidation of the Imam's authority began only with the emigration of the then Imam, Aga Khan I, to Bombay in 1845. The next six decades, approximately, were marked by expressions of dissent which came to be successfully surmounted,[10] and an Indian Ismaili community, cherishing the Ginanic tradition, and emerging with renewed strength, was eventually set on a new, distinctive stage in its history.

These historical characteristics have significant implications for the Ginans. It is worth reiterating that the focus of the present work is on the poetry, not on its history, nor on the history of the movements associated with it. But two significant implications may be noted in passing. First, *historicity* is the overwhelming feature of the Ginanic tradition. It is only right to view it as proceeding in step with the continuities and discontinuities marking the evolution of the community itself. It is not surprising that the Ginanic corpus has been interpreted, organised and appropriated differently, by different groups or in different periods in the broad history of the tradition.

Secondly, both the historical and the poetic points of view require to be distinguished from a theological treatment of this corpus. Canonisation of the material in the Ginans, an approach which converts them into a timeless corpus immune from such adaptations as were called for by ongoing history, is untenable from a historical point of view. It is, in fact, itself the product of specific historical circumstances, deserving of critical analysis in their own right.

Given the major crises to which the movement inspired by the Ginanic tradition was subjected, it is remarkable how a unified community eventually emerged with an enduring loyalty to the primary symbols of faith represented in this literature of singular beauty and power. When, at length, the Ismaili community in India, drawing inspiration from its heritage, embarked on the very different track of modernisation in the last century, at the urging of the then Imam, Aga Khan III (in whom, incidentally, the office of Imam and Pir had been formally united, henceforth strengthening the undelegated authority of the Imamate), the spiritual and secular sentiments of the community, far from colliding, proved supremely complementary.

The poetry in the Ginans had given expression to the ultimate verities of the human condition: the meaning of life; the values by which it ought to be guided; the pathos of death; and the hope, beyond death, of salvation and fulfilment. In the Ginans the community had an inexhaustible fount of ever-renewed religious experience. Their melodic words consoled the heart amidst the travails of life. To the world-weary soul, they held out the hope of inner, beatific enlightenment. Now, with the advent of modernity, came a very different imperative: a world-affirming pursuit of commercial success and prosperity; organisation of community affairs along modern, bureaucratic lines, after the model of a constitution (itself a modern concept *par excellence*); and an active discipline of mind and body answering to the principles of modern science and education. No two worlds could have been more disparate. Yet they were efficiently harmonised. This is itself a development of great interest, deserving something like a Weberian analysis. But it is, of course, a separate subject from that of the present work.

The Imamshahis have had a less happy history. The Ginanic heritage became assimilated, in their case, to a static traditionalism. And the community came to be splintered, unfortunately, into manifold factions.

Meanwhile, in the Ismaili community, composition of Ginans continued in the centuries following Imamshah's death. The Ginans which are attributed to subsequent figures do not differ from those of their predecessors in content, form, poetic merit, or popularity. A tradition within the Indian Ismaili community formally distinguishes figures from Imamshah onwards, whom it calls 'Saiyads', from the foregoing 'Pirs', a title which it interprets as indicating formal appointment by the Imam. It is reasonable to assume, however, that this distinction reflects both the consolidation of a central authority and a measure of accompanying bureaucratisation. The very notion of 'official' legitimation presupposes a literate, bureaucratic organisation. The effective crystallisation of such an ethos may safely be assumed to have occurred over time, and later rather than earlier. It is interesting to note, for example, that the Lalji Devraj editions retain, from the Khojki manuscripts, the term 'Pir' in the 'signature' verses of Imamshah's Ginans, and of some of his successors. Simultaneously, the editorial introductions to the reprints of these editions, while retaining these allusions, assert the status of their authors as 'Saiyads'. This clearly shows the co-existence of discourses from different historical periods and different socio-political contexts.

One has to guard, therefore, against a latter-day, anachronistic projection of formal clarities available only in periods dominated by legal and bureaucratic rationality, to earlier, pre-modern times. In this as in other questions relating to the corpus, a historical point of view is helpful, indeed essential, to bear in mind. These facts have at least two further implications which, in this brief introduction, can be noted only in a nutshell. First, they warrant a reiteration of the *historicity* of the tradition – its evolution and adaptation, in response to critical events, over time. Secondly, they constitute a warning against canonisation. The Ginans must be seen as a literary tradition, with merits which are poetic rather than theological, and which, moreover, have been subject to varying appropriation in different contexts over time.

Most of the Saiyads who appear as the authors of Ginans in the centuries following the death of Imamshah were descended from him or from the other children of Pir Hasan Kabirdin.[11] Of the seventeen such figures whose poetry is included in the sources used here, it will suffice to mention only the three whose Ginans have been translated in the present work. They are: Saiyad Gulmalishah, Saiyad Mohamedshah and Imam-Begum.

Saiyad Gulmalishah (or Pir Gulmalishah as he is named in his Ginans) lived in the village of Kera, in Kutch. He was one of the group called 'Kaḍiwālā Saiyads' who enjoyed immense authority in the community, and ruled its affairs. Saiyad Gulmalishah was a notably ascetic, austere figure. Much respected as a dervish, he was also esteemed by Hindus, and appears to have had close relationships with Yogis in the region. One of his Ginans (included in this volume) emphasises the brevity of life and the futility of worldly glory, in words and a melody which have a hauntingly bleak beauty.

Saiyad Mohamedshah (not to be confused with Imamshah's son), also of Kera, lived in the time of Imam Khalilullah (the father of Aga Khan I). He seems an attractive personality, nicknamed *dullā*, i.e. 'prince' or 'bridegroom', due to his reputed fondness for travelling in pomp, with a huge retinue and fanfare. He appears to have been a man with many facets – a spiritual outlook, worldly statesmanship (he was respected as a mediator by the princes of the realm), and a healthy scepticism towards superstitious beliefs. He is believed to have died in 1813.

Imam-Begum, the last in the line of the major composers of the Ginans, and the only known female figure in this class, spent most of her life in or near Bombay, but is believed to have died in Karachi any time from the third quarter of the nineteenth century to the beginning of the twentieth. Like the Kaḍiwālā Saiyads, to whose line she probably belonged, she seems to have been an interesting, even enigmatic character about whom, however, tantalisingly little is known. She was a contemporary of Aga Khan I, with whom she is once said to have had a misunderstanding, though she was retained in his patronage. Imam-Begum composed a small number of Ginans of great beauty, especially notable for their imploring tenderness and meditative intimacy.[12] Evidently, she was also an accomplished player of the fiddle (*sāraṅgī*) and sang her hymns to the accompaniment of this instrument.

A word needs to be said, to conclude this section, on the script in which the Ginans were written, and the process by which they came to be published in Gujarati. Once again, this information is already contained in the scholarly studies mentioned above. What follows is a very brief recapitulation of these facts. It is the unanimous opinion of scholars that the Ginans were first transmitted as an oral tradition. It is not known whether at least some manuscripts may have existed simultaneously – the earliest copy identified so far is dated 1736.[13] The manuscripts were all written in a special script, Khojki, which was known only to members of the community. Pre-dating the modern Devnagri script, it was apparently used by 'Hindus of Sind and Punjab for purposes of commerce'.[14] Around the turn of the last century, a large number of manuscripts from areas as far apart as Kathiawad, Kutch, Sind, Punjab, Gwadar and Muscat were assembled in Bombay. An Ismaili individual called Mukhi Lalji Devraj seems to have been officially entrusted to collate, edit and publish the content of the hundreds of manuscripts gathered by him. This he accomplished through his single-handed efforts over more than a decade. They were initially all published in Khojki, for dissemination within the Khoja community. A common practice was to publish the long works in separate or combined volumes and the shorter ones, in groups of a hundred hymns each, labelled simply, *So Ginan*: 'A Hundred Ginans'. Apparently once the Ginans were

edited and standardised, a large number of the surviving
manuscripts were destroyed.[15] Soon thereafter, the texts were also
published in Gujarati script, usually in volumes now separated
according to authorship.

Having noted the traditions surrounding the Ginans, and their
formal features, we should now look at some salient characteristics
of their content.

IV

I do not propose to approach the content of the Ginans by
enumerating their doctrines. Most of the scholars who have
worked on the Ginans (cited here) do just this. Intending to
illuminate the literature, they extract the tenets and practices to
which it might allude. Most also like to classify the Ginans by
theme and ritual function. I, for one, avoid this practice, believing
it to be misguided. Extraction of ingredients is a normal
procedure so long as the thing is a quarry, not a building, from
which it will not do to separate brick from mortar. It can work with
a mixture, not a compound. The point is that the Ginans are a
religious literature, not a compendium of religious beliefs, nor a
manual of religious ceremonies. And as for the practice of
classifying them according to the days, times or occasions on
which they might be sung, it is worth noting that only a few Ginans
refer to specific occasions or rites; when they do so, they only
allude to them, and pass on to narrate any number of other
subjects in their characteristic, free-ranging way. Moreover, they
do not themselves indicate their use for these occasions except in
a few cases and then too in rudimentary clues. It is obvious, then,
that categorisation along these lines in secondary scholarship is
prompted by actual, organised and probably latter-day practice.
Such practice may alter and evolve within the space of a
generation. Now, literature is one thing; its organised utilisation
in a communal context, in a specific time and place, another. It is
important to distinguish these. In any case, to place the emphasis
on one allusion (say, to a festival or a rite) rather than another
(say, a moral principle) is to say less about the literature than
about the commentary. And one can only wonder whether the
preference for classifying the poetry by doctrinal content or by
practical organisation – rather than, say, by poetic attributes, or

symbolic content – does not show the bias, peculiar to contexts different from that of the literature itself, for theological conceptualisation in the one case, and bureaucratic sociology in the other.[16]

This point is not hard to appreciate if one reflects on the nature of the relationship which obtains, in religious poetry, between its religious and poetic elements. Unlike theology, poetry *uses* doctrines. It does not propose them as in a creed, nor defend or justify them. Even in didactic poetry (a description which applies easily to the Ginans) – so long as it is good enough poetry, and not merely a poetic decoration of prose – religious ideas are *material* for the poetry. Nothing in this should be understood as an argument against the absolute importance of religious ideas in poetry inspired by religious commitment. The point is that the ideas do not take the form of doctrine. They are the subject-matter, not the topic, of the poetry.

In sum, I do not propose to go down the dubious path of re-stating in conceptual and discursive terms what the Ginans state in their own way – in narrative, symbolic, mythological terms. That kind of 'translation' is something of a transgression. Usually, such discursive restatement is made without consciousness of the fact. As it happens, the restatement always involves, to a greater or lesser extent, a replacement – that is, of one mode of thinking by another.

It is inadvisable, therefore, to treat the literature as a vehicle for propositions of belief and practice – as if these were the vital organs, and the lyrical and poetic aspects, the flesh around them. What is incorrectly called doctrine in this case is really the symbolic and mythological content of the poetry. I shall take only one of the symbols – the presentation of 'Ali, the first Shia Imam, as an *avatār* – in order to show what it means to treat this idea as symbolic or mythical, and why it should not be treated in any other way. But it will be convenient to approach this via a consideration of the difference between myth and history, a question prompted by the issue over the authorship of the Ginans mentioned above. This will also pave the way to the other topics which follow.

I believe that the impasse encountered in the contradiction between tradition and scholarship over the history of the Ginanic texts has its roots in a higher-order issue, namely the varying modes of reality characteristic, respectively, of mythical and historical thinking. It is, I believe, a lack of adequate attention to this level of philosophical or epistemological inquiry, which is responsible for what is otherwise a sterile controversy. The disagreement cannot be resolved by deciding in favour of one position as against another. The problem lends itself only to being dissolved, not solved. And the means to such resolution lies in this higher-order reflection.

There is no doubt that like any literature belonging to a period or place lacking in reliable, objective documentation, literature which might well have begun and been transmitted orally, and which may include the biographical and other details vulnerable to critical, scientific scrutiny – like any such literature, the Ginans are a legitimate object of textual analysis. The results of such research may plausibly lead to conclusions at variance with tradition, although such inferences must be drawn with care, and with due check on speculative imagination (which in this case, where so much remains unknown, may present a well-nigh irresistible temptation). That a good number of Ginans commemorate earlier founding-events rather than report them directly and contemporaneously is a reasonable conclusion to draw. Moreover, as mentioned above, the Ginanic tradition reflects vicissitudes of a continuing history. Despite all this, however, there is no justification for ignoring the voice of tradition, nor for treating it as an inherently direct antagonist to the point of view of critical history.

A clue to this controversy is to be found not in the actual conclusions of historical criticism, but in what we might for now simply describe (however inexactly) as its 'tone'. In rejecting traditional materials as of doubtful value (if not worse), and attributing their unsoundness to their legendary or fanciful character, the tone is clearly derogatory. This should prompt us to ask: whence this derogatory tone? What is the model of knowledge which extols historical truth in such terms as to deny reality of any kind to ideas lacking in historical truth?

My general point of view on this issue may be summarised as follows. Historical research proceeds according to its own rules of inquiry; its criteria of what counts as evidence; its rules for deciding the degree of its soundness as evidence, and for a reconstruction of the past on this basis. But historical scholarship is wrong when it dismisses the language of tradition. Both are a means to truth, but of different types. And both are susceptible to dogmatic distortion. Under the influence of modern academic culture, we are more willing to associate 'irrationalism' with traditional beliefs, than with scholarship, which in modern history has always basked in the reflected glory of the natural sciences. The truth, however, is not so agreeably one-sided. The 'rationality' of research, carried in a certain direction, can end up as irrationalism; and the narratives carried in a communal tradition have their own logic, their own rationality. Every discipline of knowledge is founded on a number of basic principles. Sometimes these become a master rather than a servant. Every organised method of inquiry has a blind spot; it is, in fact, part of its foundation. For this reason, unless critical inquiry remains self-critical, it runs the risk of dogmatism. And a usual consequence of this is a diminished appreciation of other points of view, including the 'ordinary' points of view in a society. It is like the limitation of an x-ray photograph: even as it highlights, through a play of opacity and transparency, what the naked eye cannot see, it blots out of view all that the naked eye *can* see: the beauty and the horror, so to speak, of human physicality.

It is worth asking, therefore, what kind of purchase on reality is obtained by historical criticism applied to religious tradition, whose bread and butter consists of mythical narratives, moral allegories, legendary tales of demons and deities. The historian, looking for a certain type of fact – let us simply say 'historical fact' – wages war against these ways of thinking. He does this in his bid for an account of 'what really happened'. Of this, he sees the religious narratives as rival accounts, requiring to be challenged – and subdued. When history turns doctrinaire, it is not for being over-zealous in pursuit of 'what really happened' – for in science there can be no such thing as too much rigour – but in forgetting that its 'reality' is different from the reality of the object of religious faith.

What is the mode of being of a character in history, as distinguished, say, from a character in epic poetry, legendary sagas, or scriptural narratives? History tells us of people who 'really' existed – 'really' here means people of whom one could give 'realistic' details, such as dates of birth and death, life-events, activities, travels, achievements and failures, quirks of personality and temperament. The characters assume 'objective existence' on the basis of contemporary (or near-contemporary) reports and records. The historian's characters are imagined, as it were, as publicly observable at the time in question. His own contemporary public world serves as a model on the basis of which the historian looks for similarly public individuals in the past (after due allowance for differences of time and culture). In an essential sense, his characters are 'personalities'.

By contrast, characters in religious literature are figures rather than personalities. They have a different function from that of historical characters, and answer to different objectives or motivations. The historian seeks the intellectual satisfaction of figuring out why individuals in the past (who he reasonably believes would have been recognised as such by their contemporary public) looked, behaved and turned out as they did. It is not a different task, essentially, from understanding people in general. The historian seeks to understand people (and the world inhabited and built by people) in the manner of science, i.e., 'objectively'. It is not for nothing that we regard history as a social science.

The figures of religious narratives are part of the self, the spiritual substance, of the people for whom they carry authority. This is not true of the relation of historical characters to a writer or reader of history. The historian's mind is a spectator's mind. It achieves contact in and through distance. Both contact and distance are essential for achieving the understanding, or rather, the explanation that he seeks. Myth, on the other hand, obliterates distance. The difference runs deep and strong, and along several fronts. The protagonists of mythical narratives, who are usually larger than life and have supernatural attributes, are magnified representations of the self, or the potential self. Through the deities venerated in Ancient Persia, Greece, or India, through kings, sages and noble heroes in societies everywhere, through the prophets and apostles of the Semitic faiths when these are not viewed historically but mythically (or 'mystically'), the 'I' comes into its own. It becomes, and becomes ever more fully, itself. It becomes what lies within it to become.

If, then, myth spurns normal time and space, if it seems to ignore the scruples of science, it is not because it is bad history, but because it is other than history. If it seems to 'lack' the objectivity proper to science, this is because it possesses richness of another kind. It cannot be 'objective' because it is one of the means by which (in a traditional culture) subjectivity comes into being. This is illustrated very well in its sense of time. The time of the historian is serial time, the time of the clock. Mythical time is the time of the soul. The former proceeds externally to oneself. (Where it affects one intimately, as in certain types of severe illness, it changes its character.) The latter type of time extends into one's interiority. Mythical narratives characteristically invoke huge spans of time. Theirs are the cosmic ages, cycles of creation and dissolution, the aeons through which ordeals and dramas of redemption and damnation are played out. But these huge tracts of time are not the centuries and millennia of a historical calendar. It would be equally true to say of mythical time that it is every time, and that it is timelessness. The sense of an immemorial past which we get in mythical narratives – the sense of a 'long ago', a 'once upon a time' – is the expression of a distance felt within the human condition, in a here and now. The mythical sense of origin is a sense of ongoing foundation. Its idea of an ancient lapse stems from the sense of a present infirmity. And its hope of a future fulfilment is hope in a present-day ideal. If science confers the gift of knowledge, myth bestows fullness of existence.

Thanks to the spectacular advances of science in modern history, we tend to look upon non-scientific modes of thought with a certain condescension. Thus, when historians consider myth, what they notice most is the absence of ways of thought peculiar to their own approach. They see the *absence* as a *lack*. This is where history passes into historicism, science into dogma. The drive for knowledge is tainted by a drive for conquest, for domination. In mocking the lack of historical veracity in myth, history ignores its independent scope and purpose. By casting it in its own terms, meeting it only on its own ground, it readies it for subjugation – much like a creature of water (say, a crocodile) might vanquish a land beast (say, a buffalo) by first hauling it into the water, where of course it is no longer its real self.

The very term 'myth' carries the scars of this modern battle. It is negatively defined, placing the accent on what it is not rather than what it is. Originally, *mythos* simply meant 'tale' or 'speech'. Subsequently, it acquired a negative flavour through counter-definition. The first rival of myth was philosophy, championed by Plato, who grants to myth, nonetheless, the function of a veiled presentation of truth. Much later, with the advent of Enlightenment rationalism and positivist science, myth became synonymous with falsehood. Lately, however, social science, keen to shake off the positivist legacy, has sought to re-create the old sense of the word. The history of the word, thus, is a beleaguered one. Here, I use the term 'myth' only (as I suspect some other writers also do) for lack of a better alternative to date.

The above points could be put into academic shorthand by saying that what is vital in historical research relying primarily on religious texts, is for textual criticism to be integrated with the perspectives of anthropology and philosophy of history. I have so far avoided this academic phraseology lest the impression be conveyed that what is at stake is no more than a decision as to which academic discipline one is to call upon here; whereas academic disciplines, as everyone who is not enslaved to them knows, are only conventions. Moreover, to follow a discipline is not an assured path to the perspective which it promises. And lastly, like all specialised discourse, conventional terminology may produce the misleading impression that the relevant issue is one of procedure, rather than basic vision.

This philosophical digression was necessary, I believe, because it has been absent, even by way of background, from critical, historical scholarship on the Ginans to date. Despite the undeniable contribution of this scholarship, it has seldom, if ever, benefited from higher-order reflection, of the type represented, in academic disciplines, by subjects like philosophical anthropology, philosophy of history and literary criticism.

Applying these principles to the portraits of the Pirs in the Ginans, the following points may be made by way of summary.

Textual criticism, as the means to the historical re-construction of a literature like the Ginans, must be ever conscious that the content of these texts is motivated by, and serves purposes other than those of factual information. The figures which appear in it are archetypal rather than empirically imagined. They are there as much as expressions or symbols of the sacred universe as memories of a bygone past. Such memories as there are, are loaded with archetypal significance and are not therefore in the nature, primarily, of a factual record. They are there not, as we say, 'for the record', but as part of the collective imagination of a living community. They are the means through which a traditional community interprets its foundations, its mission and its destiny. This is what historical scholarship must *systematically* recognise. Rather than looking down on communal tradition as a poor relative, an inferior version of itself, it must, on intellectual grounds, appreciate its social and psychological function, the integrity of its vision.

It must be admitted that most scholars of religious texts appreciate the difference between fact and belief, and this appreciation is to some extent reflected in scholarship on the Ginans.[17] All too often, however, this concession is vitiated by a view of myth and legend which sees them as occupying the same ground as history. This view makes it impossible for a textual scholar to see the two activities of mind in any other way than as competitive interpretations of the same phenomenon. Thus, his left hand is quick to withdraw what his right hand is willing to grant. As the prize is assumed to be 'real' facts, the two accounts come to be seen as mutually exclusive, one being true, the other false. My argument here is that the historical point of view must rather be subsumed into a wider perspective, along the lines indicated above.

But, if all this can be said in fair criticism of a one-sided reverence for historical fact, equally vigorous criticism must be directed at traditionalism. In insisting that the narratives in a tradition be taken at face value, traditionalism shows itself to be the mirror-image of historicism. What they both share is literalism. Only, the traditionalist is on weaker grounds than the textual scholar, for the latter has critical method on his side. By contrast, a traditionalist's insistence on the literal truth of his beliefs is at bottom no more than an assertion. The onus of proof is thus shifted onto him. As he has no means of proving his claims, he can only assert them; he can only do so, in other words, dogmatically.

In this way, a literal interpretation of tradition turns out to be self-destructive. By literalising the language of tradition, one succeeds only in trivialising it. The champions of tradition, therefore, have as much need, as scholars, to appreciate the composite dimension of analysis being urged here. They too must understand that the language of religious narratives is (in the psychoanalytic sense) 'over-determined': it has many functions, and few (if any) of them are literally referential.

The nature of mythopoetic language is a vital key to understanding the conception not only of the Pirs, but also of the Ismaili Imam. Before elaborating on this, however, it will be interesting to consider an example of the treatment of Ginans along the lines criticised above. The best example is the work of

Vladimir Ivanow, the first Orientalist to study the subject. His work has the added advantage, moreover, of highlighting a further, twofold problem in Ginanic studies: the tendency to compare the Ginans with Arabo-Persian Ismailism (normally to the disadvantage of the former); and to read what is essentially an Indian vernacular literature through a filter of Arabo-Persian concepts.[18]

In criticising Ivanow, one must not be uncharitable, nor begrudge his undoubted contribution. He was a pioneer of Ismaili studies in the Orientalist field, and showed all the perseverance and resourcefulness required in a new enterprise. If I criticise Ivanow below, it is with two qualifying considerations in mind. First, I criticise not the quality of his work but the view of knowledge dominant in his day, which he had unconsciously imbibed. Secondly, I treat this view as *representative* of this type of scholarship in general. Historical treatments of the Ginans – and much historical writing in the Orientalist field as a whole – continue to display similar characteristics to Ivanow's. Indeed, Ivanow's limitations are if anything more excusable than those of contemporary Orientalists sharing this approach, as the topics of myth, popular culture, etc., have received much more systematic attention and articulation since his day.

When, after a long career of research in Arabic and Persian Ismaili texts, Ivanow turned his attention to Ginanic literature (through informants, as he did not read Indian languages), he was dismayed by finding in it qualities opposite to everything he admired in the former. The Ginans, he complained, cared little for chronology and the correct perspective on events. Lacking a 'historical sense', they gave full vent to 'fantasy'.[19]

It is, of course, far from self evident that Aristotelian or Neoplatonic philosophy (strongly represented in Fatimid Ismailism) has transcendent superiority over folk or mythological literature. But to Ivanow this went without saying. So, he looked down on those aspects of the Ginans which did not fit this assumed model of perfection, putting them down, at worst, to the alleged primitiveness of Hindu mentality, and at best, to the Pirs' concession to this mentality for purposes of conversion.[20]

If there was any doubt of the source of the bias in Ivanow's attitude to the Ginans, a further illustration will suffice to prove the point. Referring to the *Jannatpuri* of Imamshah (mentioned above), Ivanow laments that it is not like the 'admirable *Safarnama*' of the Persian philosopher Nasir-i Khusraw, in which he 'sanely and sobermindedly described' what he saw on his journeys through the Islamic lands.[21] We are much better able in our time to see the absurdity of this comparison. But it is worth reflecting further on a difference between the two works. The *Safar-nama*, we could say, is a tribute to a great mind whose greatness is an ability to see reality without religious or mythical interference – to see it objectively. What is interesting about the *Jannatpuri* is precisely the opposite: its wealth of religious imagination. Imagination is the poorer when it is 'sober'. And sometimes it stands to gain, rather than lose, when it is 'insane' – when there is method in the madness, rather than madness for lack of method.

Of Nasir-i Khusraw, one could say that in a world whose mental landscape was defined by religion, he was to a high degree – to adapt the words of the great literary critic, Erich Auerbach, about Dante – an observer 'of the secular world'. A Ginan like the *Jannatpuri*, on the other hand, calls to mind the mythical aspects of *The Divine Comedy*. So does a work like Pir Sadardin's *Bāwan Ghāṭi*, which is a graphic depiction of the torments of hell.

It is only an uncritical, and as it happens, narrow bias in favour of conceptual and philosophical prose, at the expense of mythopoetic literature, which hinders one's appreciation of such works. Ginanic literature has thus had a raw deal from authors whose brand of rationalism is in fact an unexamined prejudice. (It is significant that during Ivanow's scholarly career, positivism was still a dominant force in philosophy of science). And although Ivanow (like so many specialist scholars) was not familiar with general philosophical issues, nor the philosophy of science, he could not have escaped their influence – any more than we today are able to escape, unless we are critically conscious, the influence of contemporary dogmas.

Ivanow's treatment of the Ginans also draws our critical attention to a common assumption, namely that since they are Ismaili literature, they must be a reincarnation of Persian (Nizari), if not Fatimid, Ismailism. But the Ginans are far too genuine a literary creation to be a mere dress for doctrines formulated in another time and place. The habit of subordinating the Ginans to Arabo-Persian Ismailism, by interpreting them, in the face of all internal evidence, as a mere vehicle for the latter, dies hard.[22] It is quite astonishing, for instance, how automatically most scholarly studies of the Ginans describe the mission of the Pirs as *da'wa*, and the Pirs themselves as *da'is*. The use of these Arabic terms in

English writing on an Indian literature is in itself sufficient to make us pause. But one's astonishment is compounded when we observe that the Ginans never use either of these terms. What might explain this widespread paradox?

The *da'wa* was, no doubt, a fundamental institution in Fatimid Ismailism, and the *da'i* had a defined position in the cosmic and religious hierarchy proposed in the Fatimid scheme, and repeated, with some radical revisions, in its Nizari sequel. Scholars who treat the Ginanic tradition as an extension or offshoot of this arrangement betray a tendency to essentialise, to universalise, the institution and doctrine of the *da'wa*, and to treat it as definitive of 'Ismailism' as such. In doing so, they fail to attend consciously to the absence of this institution, of the idea as well as the practice, in Ismaili communities in other phases of history. This is not to say that the Ginanic tradition did not *originate* in a process of conversion (of whose period and extent there is still a lot to be discovered). But origin is not essence. Without digressing too far into philosophical analysis, we may highlight three potentially misleading perspectives in subsuming the Ginanic tradition into the historically and geographically specific ideology and institution of the *da'wa*. First is the 'essentialisation' just mentioned. Second is the fact that in its historical preoccupation – its concern to find the point of *origin* – this way of speaking ends up being unhistorical by assuming, without question, that ideologies and institutions conceivable and feasible in a political state (or quasi-state) would also exist and make sense in other social contexts. (What we have here, in other words, is a historical interpretation insufficiently schooled in sociology). Thirdly, this way of speaking about the Ginanic literature takes up a vantage-point *external* to the literature. Taken together, these attitudes may be found in academic discourse in the Ismaili (and indeed Islamic) context more generally. In all such instances, there is an excess of one type of history at the expense of another, namely, sociologically sensitive history. And the history which is carried too far in this connection is also deficient *as history*. For, by presuming timeless, monolithic abstraction, it undermines the very point of view essential to a historical consciousness.

The inter-relationship of Arabic, Persian and Indian Ismailism – I put it advisedly in this form, rather than 'Ismailism in the Arab, Persian and Indian lands' – requires not only more finely balanced, but also more subtly conceived formulation. Moreover, what may be said about Ismailism in this respect is no different, in essence, from what must be said about Islam in general. Before we address this issue, however, we need to complete our discussion of mythopoetic thought by considering the depiction of the Ismaili Imam in the Ginans.

V

That the figure of 'Ali, or his descendant (Ismaili) Imam, is central to the Ginans, is not in doubt. He is both the addressee and the theme – spoken to and spoken about. This twofold linguistic usage is significant, for it indicates that while the figure of the Imam exists in geographical and public space – in Iran, as history tells us – he also exists in the collective psychology and imagination of the community to which the Ginans were given. The Imam's presence in Iran is distant enough from the majority of the followers in the towns and villages of the Subcontinent for him, as well as his residence, to be conceived in mytho-symbolic terms. It is, in effect, another world: and in the positive sense of the word, an imaginary (or imaginative) world. Moreover, no historical information about the past Imams, 'Ali b. Abu Talib, or about the Prophet, is given. They are figures, not historical personalities – figures in a cosmic drama of creation and salvation. There are certainly allusions to contemporary Imams: Qasim Shah and Nizar in Pir Shams' Ginans (the difference in the likely lifetimes of these two figures being one of the arguments in favour of an element of evolution in the texts); and '*Sri*' Islamshah in Pir Sadardin and Pir Hasan Kabirdin. But these allusions are devoid of circumstantial detail. Nor, for that matter, is the Alid descent of the Imam, so emphatically documented in Fatimid texts, detailed in the Ginans. The contemporary Imam is implicitly identified with 'Ali without any apparent need to trace the link historically.[23] All this underlines the abstract, archetypal, spiritual (rather than physical) dimension of the Imam (as well as the great, early Pirs, who are also, as mentioned above, mythical, cosmic figures). The imagination, unconstrained by physical encounter, is left totally free. It apprehends sacred reality through typical representations which transcend literal, physical identification.

It is for this reason that the translation of the term *avatār* (Sanskrit *avatāra*), applied in the Ginans to the figure of 'Ali (or the Imam) as 'incarnation' is unsatisfactory. 'Incarnation' means embodiment, the manifestation of spirit in the guise of flesh. Although we have very little, if any, information about the historical Jesus which will stand up to historical scrutiny, and the figure of Christ therefore provides full freedom to the imagination to conceive him according to personal or social need, Christian doctrine has made the Incarnation – God made flesh – a central pillar of the faith. But the myths surrounding the notion of *avatāra*, whose etymology implies 'descent', do not emphasise bodily incorporation of the divine. Even the concreteness of the notion in the Sanskrit texts remains imaginative: it is a pictorial representation, unattended by the insistence that this be accepted as referring to a historical life or career. The difference, though subtle, is theologically far-reaching. Moreover, in the Ginans the concept of the *avatār* undergoes further rarefaction. They regularly allude to the nine *avatāras* of ancient Indian mythology, in which the tenth *avatār*, named *kalki*, is still awaited. The Ginans announce this last manifestation (for which they use the alternative name, *nakalaṅki*, or *nikalaṅki*, with its additional meaning of the 'spotless' or 'blemish-less' – the 'immaculate'), to have already occurred in the appearance of 'Ali or his successor-Imam.[24] Moreover, these references are no more than allusions. They are free of the picturesque, often lurid detail of the narratives around them which we find, for instance, in the *Puranas*. Unless one makes this comparison, the relative sparseness of concrete detail in the Ginans' treatment of this concept is apt to be overlooked. Once this is appreciated, however, the possibility suggests itself that the Ginans are *using* this allusion as a means rather than an end – the end being a logical transition to the new faith. In the process, however, the other consequence, the spiritualisation just mentioned, also comes into force.

Failure to understand this point can easily lead to a misinterpretation of Ginanic doctrine. From the point of view of 'orthodox' Islam, these allusions may be seen as inconsistent with the doctrine of the transcendence of God. Intellectual analysis has no place for judgements of correct or incorrect doctrine, of orthodoxy or heterodoxy. For such judgements reflect battles for power and dominance among competing groups in a society through the vehicle of ideology. As such, they can have no scientific or objective basis. But insofar as such judgements are symptomatic of social or historical struggles, and to the degree that they have implications for a theoretical understanding of religion, they deserve intellectual analysis and criticism. In the present section, we shall confine ourselves to this theoretical issue.

The theoretical objection to the orthodox view may be stated quite simply: it ignores the reality of religious imagination. Among modern scholars, Henry Corbin is perhaps the only one to have systematically pursued the topic of creative imagination in mystical faith. (Though he has confined himself to Arabo-Persian Islam, his remarks are general enough to have broader relevance to Islam, and indeed to religion as a whole). It is sufficient to glance at one or two of the dominant concepts in his study of the great Muslim mystic, Ibn al-ʿArabi (1165–1240), to see the central role of creative imagination in all religious experience.

Corbin's commentary places emphasis on the character of the Divine Object as an *appearance*, a manifestation (*mazhar*). The eye of faith perceives the divine object in and through a form, a symbol, a figuration. Most striking, in this connection, is the phrase, 'the God created in the faiths'.[25] This phrase emphasises the divine object as a *phenomenon* conceived in the mode of faith accessible to the believer. Although Corbin was resolutely opposed to the view that the figuration of the sacred is historically conditioned, his contribution is not incompatible with such a view. Perhaps the most instructive model for an approach which, unlike Corbin's, gives full acknowledgement to the role of history, sociology and psychology in the representation of the sacred (without, however, reducing the object of faith to any of these dimensions), is to be found in the work of Paul Ricoeur. While having all the pertinent secular disciplines at his command, Ricoeur also affirms the integrity of the object of faith, the 'Wholly Other' which, however – and this point is of great theological interest – 'annihilates its otherness' in its self-presentation in human culture.[26]

The concept of *avatāra*, then, is one example, among numerous others, to be observed universally, of the 'God created in the faiths'. The emphasis here is on epiphany, i.e. appearance, manifestation. It is a travesty of this idea to interpret it literally as physical incarnation. This misunderstanding is all the more likely to occur when the concept is addressed in isolation from the entire text of the Ginans, and from the world in which they were first current. When we look at the Ginans in a theoretical light, it becomes amply clear that the figures of the Imam and the major

Pirs, considered *phenomenologically,* belong less to material history, than to a poetics of the sacred.

Of course, orthodox discourse ignores such subtleties. In this connection, it is surely ironic that the conception of the Divine Being in Ash'ari-Hanbali orthodoxy is thoroughly anthropomorphic, insisting on a literal acceptance of the physical or quasi-physical attributes of God presented in the Quran. Besides, the orthodox denial of religious imagination – a denial in which practice contradicts theory – is unsustainable except at a heavy price, an obliviousness, namely, to the immense variety of religious experience to be found in human history.

There is, however, a further point to be considered. Misunderstanding of Ginanic content arises not only due to a neglect of these subtleties, but also out of a belief in its supposedly 'Hindu' character. (The concept of *avatārs,* for instance is clearly Vaishnavite). How, it is sometimes asked, can these concepts be termed 'Islamic'?

VI

It is possible to show that this last question is misplaced, and that what it deserves is not an answer, but critical deconstruction. To this end, we need to take note of a fact curiously ignored in many historical accounts of Islam. The history of Islam is a history of a large number of local or regional cultures. This is as true of the Arab lands and Iran, as of Islamic Spain, Turkey, Indonesia or Africa. The idea of a culture-free Islam is an abstraction from historical reality. Every religious tradition creates and recreates itself through an ever-shifting synthesis of inherited and contemporary ideas. In the Indian Subcontinent, the result was a distinctive blend of indigenous and erstwhile foreign motifs which, once they had come together, formed a seamless whole. It is only ideological self-consciousness which sifts among the elements, distinguishing 'Hindu' from 'Muslim', and seeks to suppress, minimise, or to explain away some of them in an apologetic vein. For the earlier community, free from such self-consciousness, there are no 'components', there is only an integrated culture. Likewise, there is no need felt, in the former context, to define the faith in hard and fast, global categories. The anxiety to *define* at all arises when there is a surrounding polemic in terms of orthodoxy and heterodoxy. Such debates make a people look at their beliefs from the outside. Ideological self-consciousness results from the absorption of an exterior point of view. Where such environmental pressures are absent, the conditions are more favourable to an organic vision, anchored in the mental and social realities of the people. The Ginans are one such 'organic' tradition.

It must be emphasised that they are only one such tradition. The doctrinal and symbolic content of the Ginans is far from idiosyncratic. On the contrary, it has a considerable overlap with other literatures of the continent. Nothing is more misleading, therefore, than to consider the Ginans in isolation from the other literatures in the same milieu.

Many historians of Islam in the Indian Subcontinent have remarked on the characteristic form it took there in popular culture. The type of ideas we have just noted, far from being peculiar, were entirely typical. For example, among Sunnis in Bengal, the Prophet Muhammad was regarded as the 'incarnation of God himself'.[27] He was seen as the last, tenth incarnation of Vishnu, the '*avatāra* of Kali-yuga', superseding the nine previous incarnations.[28] He was the *avatāra* of the times, the wicked *kaliyuga* (the fourth and last age, according to the *Vedas*, in world-history). In Indian mytho-history, each of the *Vedas* corresponded to each of the four ages. And so popular Islam, retaining this scheme of the *yugas* and the *Vedas*, thought of the teachings of Islam as the last scripture, perfecting and superseding earlier wisdom (just as the Quran had presented itself as a successor to the God-given scriptures of the other Semitic faiths).[29]

Thus, what we find in the Ginans corresponds to the prevalent stock of ideas in popular Indian Islam at large (except in that it is 'Ali, the paradigmatic Shia Imam, who is here conceived in these terms). Even the Hindu pantheon is freely drawn upon in popular Subcontinental Islam. Thus, Bengali Sunni Muslim literature relates how the birth of the Prophet Muhammad shook and startled the king of gods, Indra, and smashed the door of heaven so that the gods, thrown into confusion, were unable to ascend to their places.[30] There is no parallel to this tale in the Ginans. But some of the elements they draw on from the indigenous milieu are again to be observed more generally in Indian Islam. A case in point are the doctrines of Yoga. These are sometimes hailed as 'the command of God', the 'eternally concealed truth'. The

Hindu scriptures, the *Puranas*, as well as the Quran are declared, in this bold claim, to be 'incapable of leading to the path of *yog*'. An uninterrupted reading of scripture for 'a hundred years' will bring the devotee no nearer the esoteric truth.[31]

Another indigenous idea retained in Indian Islam, especially among Sufi communities (e.g. in Punjab) is that of reincarnation. Again, the celebrated erotic love between Radha and lord Krishna is a standard theme in Bengali Islam (and indeed, more generally).[32] This is not to be found in the Ginans, except for very occasional references to the dalliance between Krishna and the maiden cowherds.

The type of Islam which was most congenial to indigenisation was Sufism. With its devotional focus on a person (*Pir* or *murshid*) as opposed to what Clifford Geertz has called 'scripturalism', and its emphasis on the supremacy of esoteric essence over exoteric formalism, Sufi ideas could coalesce easily with analogous strands in indigenous culture, with its reverence for the *guru*. There was likewise a major overlap between Sufi critiques of orthodoxy and the protest of the Bhakti movements against conventional religion in the name of sincere worship of the heart.[33] The Chisthi of Bijapur, for instance, drew heavily from the Bhakti tradition.[34] In this way, the result was the transposition of the all too familiar audacities of Sufism in the Arabo-Persian-Turkish contexts to the Subcontinental context. When Asim Roy points out, for instance, that the 'Bengali Muslims' adoration of the Pir was unqualified and boundless',[35] this is hardly news to anyone with the remotest familiarity with Sufism. Nor are such exclamations as the following, attributed to a Punjabi Sufi poet, Sultan Bahu (1631–91), at all atypical: True lovers of God are 'neither Hindus nor Muslims, nor do they prostrate in mosques. At every breath they see God'. The path of God remains hidden from '*pandits* and *maulavis*'. 'The *Murshid* is Makka, the seeker, the pilgrim, and love I have made [my] Kaaba'. Again: 'The *Murshid* is my life, contained in every pore of mine'. Reverence for the *murshid* leads this author, typically, to describe him, as the 'Pir of Pirs', unique and incomparable in all creation. The focus on the *murshid* makes conventional religious identities relative and insignificant, so that the poet could say, 'Some have reached union in idol-houses, others have remained [unfulfilled] in mosques'.[36]

Similar sentiments are echoed now and again in other parts, and in other voices. Thus, in Bengali mystical Islam, Hindu as well as Muslim scripture were declared as 'exoteric', in comparison to mystical, 'esoteric' wisdom.[37] The devotee is urged to lay himself at his Pir's feet, for this will earn him 'greater merit than prayer' (*namaz*).[38] The Pir is to be 'served after the manner of the Lord himself'. A day spent at his feet is equivalent to pious works of 'a thousand years'. It behoves the devotee to heed the Pir's call even in the midst of prayer, for it confers far greater spiritual merits.[39] It was entirely in this vein, and in terms thoroughly typical of mysticism west of the Subcontinent, that a Bengali Sufi such as Ali Raja could praise his Pir as the 'Grace of the world, the light [*nur*] of heaven on earth, and the lamp of [his own] heart'.[40] The Pir was routinely regarded as a possessor of charismatic gifts (*barakat*) and as an interceder with God on behalf of his disciples (*murids*).[41]

Lastly, it is not surprising that in the Subcontinent, this all too typical reverence for the spiritual guide merged into indigenous idiom, so that the Pir, commonly also called Guru, came to be equated with such names of Hindu deities as Ishvara and Brahma. Thus, when another Bengali poet, Saiyad Sultan, could speak of the guru as 'the supreme Isvar, [without] equal in the three worlds', he seems to have been doing no more than repeating a standard formula in popular, mystical religion of the time.[42]

When we turn to the Ginans, therefore, we would do well to keep the general context in mind, for otherwise, appearing idiosyncratic as it is bound to do, and lacking contextual placing, their content will defy systematic understanding. This does not mean that there is no individuality in the Ginans – no differences, for instance, between some (though not all) of their content and the ideas and sentiments just quoted. Often enough, however, they are subtle, though not, on that account, any the less far reaching. One significant trait of the Ginans, for example, is that they do not *dwell* on Hindu mythological lore. This may be put more precisely in terms of the type of discourse in which it occurs. The mythology is not the *object* of Ginanic discourse; rather, it appears in a subordinate status (in syntax and meaning) to another object, which is Satpanth, Indian Ismailism. What the Ginans do share in common with the surrounding religious culture more generally, whether in its Sufi or Bhakti forms (these labels and distinctions have their limitations) is their appeal to charismatic faith as a counter-motif to orthodox formalism. This is one of the reasons for the remarkable overlaps between the literatures of different communities in this category. Between the traditions of the Sufis and the Vaishnavite poets, for instance, the commonalities are often so striking as to make differentiation between them difficult, if not pointless. To some extent, this is due to the very nature of oral traditions, which do not know the modern copyright and conventions of individual authorship. But more is obviously involved.

It seems that there was a common pool of ideas on which different communities with separate allegiances to their respective leaders drew freely, articulating a shared vision of the world. It is in such terms that we might account for the striking similarities, and in a few instances, complete identity, between some of the Ginans and the poetry of men like the famous Kabir.[43] The collection of Khojki manuscripts at Harvard's Widener Library, which originated from Indian Ismaili households, and pre-date the Lalji Devraj treatment, embrace a miscellany of items. They comprise, along with the Ginans, devotional poems by little-known Khoja poets, elegies about the martyrdom of the Alid family at Karbala, narratives of events commemorated by the Shi'a in Muharram, praise-poems about 'Ali b. Abu Talib, stories of the Prophets, some major poets of Gujarat like Narsinh Mehta, and biographies of Sufi thinkers like Ibn al-'Arabi and Jalal al-Din Rumi. This heterogeneity is entirely in keeping with the robust inter-culturalism characteristic of the mystical and devotional (as opposed to orthodox) ethos which has long prevailed in the Subcontinent. Moreover, this juxtaposition of different literary traditions in the Indian Ismaili context suggests that the Ginanic heritage had an essentially poetic status at the time in question. This belies the claim, made by some nowadays, of its 'scriptural' status in the community.[44]

There is another strand in the anti-formalism of these literatures which is worth noting here. Behind the polarity of living symbolism and formalistic belief and ritual, there lies another, significant opposition. Formal orthodoxy is given to sharp-etched boundaries between self and other, 'inside' and 'outside'. Not so mystical or devotional religion. Both the Bhakti movement within Hinduism, and Sufism within Islam, emphasising spirit over letter, worship of the essence over blind conformity to structure, conviction of mind over learning got from books, and gestures of the heart over motions of the body, reached out towards the human condition, ignoring or downplaying distinctions of caste and creed. From around the 15th to the 19th century, the Indian Subcontinent saw movements of great ferment and protest against the culture of the mullahs and the pundits. There was here a true universalism in the offing. Whether through express statements of the oneness of all creeds (as in Kabir) or through a common stock of symbols and images upon which different communities drew without ideological hesitation, the literature in this period celebrated a unitary essence hidden behind myriads of superficial differences.

From the earliest times, this universalism was under attack. The lines of battle ran along divisions of social class. Thus, among Muslims, a Persianate elite frowned upon what they saw as the heretical beliefs of the masses. In Bengal, popular preachers were torn between a desire to communicate with the masses and a reluctance to use the vernacular for this purpose.[45] These tensions were given a new lease of life in the 19th and 20th centuries, when Islamic revivalism, supported by conditions peculiar to modern states, introduced a new layer of self-consciousness in indigenous Muslim communities. Anthropological studies of Islam in Rajasthan and Haryana, for instance, bear witness to deliberate policies, in modern times, of replacing 'Hindu' elements with their 'Islamic' equivalents.[46]

As one might expect, Hindu and Islamic revivalism on the Subcontinent has bred new dichotomies and new varieties of self-consciousness. Unfortunately, the orthodoxies of dominant discourse in societies are often adopted, lock stock and barrel, by academics studying and reporting on the societies in question. Asim Roy is one of the few scholars who has criticised the glib employment of terms such as 'Hindu' and 'Muslim' by historians of the Subcontinent, who ought to know better. Such labels ought to be used with all the more caution, he suggests, because Islam in South Asia was never 'textual or doctrinal' to start with. Likewise, he has drawn attention to the distortion resulting from the assumption of a 'monolithic or a world Islam, defined essentially in textual terms of the *Sunni* orthodoxy'. Starting from this prior position, 'the empirical realities of Islamic development in a regional or local setting are viewed through the prism of this idealised and abstract norm and hence discarded as "folk" or "popular" aberrations'.[47]

It follows, further, that theological approaches to local Islam generate more heat than light. The significance of vernacular religious experience will continue to elude us as long as its sociological dimension is ignored or poorly understood.

To acknowledge the integrity of local or regional experience is also to understand the phenomenon of collective 'conversion' in a more nuanced way than has hitherto been the case. The following section provides a few preliminary remarks to this end.

VII

One dominant approach to conversion looks upon it as a swift, total substitution of one religious identity for another. Moreover, it assumes that the beliefs which are adopted remain what they were, without being affected or modified in the process. Richard Eaton has criticised this model very aptly: 'we can no longer conceptualise the phenomenon of conversion' he says, 'as early generations did, in terms of the "spread" of an essentialised tradition from point A to point B – typically, from metropolis to periphery – as though it were a substance . . . . flowing outward from some central point . . . . Rather, we should adopt the perspective of the *society actually undergoing change* and see conversion *not as passive acceptance of a monolithic, outside essence,* but as a "creative adaptation" of *the unfamiliar to what is already familiar,* a process in which the former may change to suit the latter'.[48]

This observation fits the spread of Islam from sub-Saharan Africa to South-east Asia. It helps to highlight several characteristics of this process. First, the incoming ideas or symbols are locally perceived or conceptualised. Viewed from the recipient's (rather than the transmitter's) vantage-point, they are re-moulded from the start. Thus, 'reception' is not the passive, subordinate process the word implies; it is an active, mutative operation.

Secondly, the incoming notions are lined up alongside existing ideas and symbols. In due course, they come to be interwoven, such that they cannot be told apart. (When ideologically inspired revision takes place, and the elements are re-differentiated into the old and the new, this process marks a new development rather than a recapitulation).

Thirdly, the process always results in a continuum. Over time, new layers may be added, and a re-arrangement of the parts, with a new distribution of emphases, takes place. There is always scope for evolution, though this is not necessarily unilinear.

Lastly, this process results from a group's entire historical trajectory – social, political, economic, cultural. It must not be understood solely in terms of the history of a text, but in the group's differing appropriations, its reconceptualisation, through the passage of time, of its textual heritage.

Oversimplified notions of conversion have caused these historical subtleties to be ignored. Even anthropologists are guilty. Clifford Geertz has recognised the slow, 'step by step' character of conversion to Islam, but this still assumes, as Imtiaz Ahmad rightly observes, 'a one-way process from a non-Islamic way of life to an Islamic one ....'[49] Conscious of this oversimplification, Satish Misra has insisted on a distinction between 'indigenisation' and 'Islamization', viewing them as proceeding in opposite directions.[50] Ahmad, seeking to modify this further, has proposed a view in which both processes alternate. As history shows, Islam everywhere has been 'an evolving and accumulating tradition wherein new elements have continually been absorbed and integrated from time to time'. On one hand, beliefs and practices from Islamic religious thought and culture came to be assimilated. On the other hand, beliefs and customs drawn from local, indigenous culture are 'incorporated into orthodox Islam'. It is thus, in Ahmad's view, 'a two-way process', in which what constitutes 'Islamization' has to do not with the source of ideas and customs, but with 'whether they were viewed as Islamic and therefore as basic to the definition of a group or individual as Muslim'.[51]

Still, none of this manages to capture the character of the kind of literature of which the Ginans are a part. This is for at least two reasons. First, while Ahmad has no doubt made a contribution by re-examining the notion of Islamization, he forecloses a radical re-examination of the other notion, namely 'conversion', by subsuming it under the label of 'Islamization', thus retaining the basic polarity.

Secondly, he thinks of Islam predominantly, in this context, in terms of 'scriptural sources and *Sharia* law'. This second limitation indeed accounts for the first. Yet one has only to glance at mystical Muslim movements in the history of the Subcontinent to perceive that this formulation does not describe their dynamic adequately.

The label 'Islamization' is best confined to self-consciousness in a group about its own identity as 'Muslim'. It reflects its self-definition, and self-presentation, in 'Islamic' terms. (Exactly parallel observations may be made in respect of other faiths). However, the literatures considered here, whether they are to be defined as 'mystical', 'devotional', or whatever, transcend such identity-asserting concerns. The 'conversion' to which they testify is deeper than denominational – it is at once psychological, cultural and spiritual.

The phenomenon of conversion is far more complex than routine uses of the word suggest. Sociologists of religion, wrestling with the subject, have variously proposed additional concepts such as 'adhesion', 'syncretism', etc., to reflect this complexity. But I do not believe that these terms have finally laid the difficulty of explaining this complex phenomenon to rest. Thus, the term 'syncretism' which received support from Clifford Geertz in his account of the religion of Java, has long been used in the South Asian context, and hence has also been applied to the Ginans. But as one critic has pointed out, in 'the strictest terms all religious doctrines are syncretic'.[52] Moreover, the term 'syncretism' has the disadvantage of maintaining the polarity it seeks to dissolve. Again, when one writer defines the term as a 'fusion of two or more systems of belief or ritual to form a new, unified, and harmonious system',[53] we may well wonder whether the idea of distinct 'systems' is not too neat, too abstract, in comparison with processes of local religious interaction and evolution.

If we now apply the implications of the above discussion to the history of the Ginanic literature, the following observations may be made.

First, in keeping with the above view of conversion, Ginanic literature must be seen for what it is: not the superimposition, on the Indian milieu, of Persian, still less Arabic (Fatimid) Ismailism. It is the product, rather, of an indigenous, 'organic' creativity, catalysed by a number of processes of which we do not now have records, of which one was an *initial* emigration of Arabo-Persian Ismaili ideas. But these were remoulded, assimilated, appropriated in ways characteristic of the Subcontinental milieu. The resulting ideas have their own distinctive complexion. What is preserved is the centrality, common to all branches of Ismailism, of the figure of the Imam; and secondly, perhaps, a predilection for the inward dimension of faith. The adaptation of these notions in the Ginans must be understood in the sense suggested in our discussion of 'translation' at the outset of this essay. The Ginans' is a voice speaking naturally out of its milieu, like a garden sprung from native, self-matured soil, where the saplings grafted from abroad have twined only too well with the erstwhile vegetation, and made the habitat their own.

The importance of recognising this distinctive identity must be balanced, however, by a converse emphasis. There has been a tendency to see the Ginans as the expression, *par excellence*, of Ismaili belief and practice. But they are the literature of a particular time and place, and display the culture and conditions peculiar to that setting. The Ismailis have had a varied history, and are culturally a diverse people. The fact that Indian Ismailism has a distinctive identity also means that its other historical or geographical counterparts are likewise distinct. The Ginans are not a key to 'Ismailism' as such; they are not a window to the faith in its Arabic, Persian or Central Asian manifestations. If they have sometimes been treated as such, it has been due to the incurable appetite of students of religion or culture to want a faith summed up in its entirety, spelt out in a few well-punctuated formulae. This trend was especially encouraged by the fact that Ismaili literature in these other languages was for long inaccessible. But this approach to the Ginans is a mistaken one.

Moreover, the community itself has changed. Indian Ismailis are now part of a larger cluster of Ismaili communities. Their consciousness of one another, heightened by modern mobility and communication, and their appropriation of their formative history – part and parcel of the formative history of Islam – must necessarily reflect back on their specifically Indian heritage. This cannot now be, as it once was, all-embracing. It is a unit in a larger whole. When what was once a whole becomes part of another whole, it is inevitably seen with a different sense of proportion.

The Indian Ismailis have not only undergone, but embraced historical change. It is one thing to appreciate a heritage, quite another to use it to infer the beliefs and sentiments of a people at a different historical juncture from the original. Even though the heritage has lived on in the Indian community and (with less immediacy) in its diaspora, the complexion of the community has altered profoundly in its economic, organisational and cultural spheres. This has been due to the joint impact of history and the historically sensitive leadership of the present Imam and his predecessor with regard to all their followers. When an old literature lives on in a society which has crossed the long bridge between tradition and modernity, attitudes to the literature are bound to evolve. It is now part of a larger whole where at one time it would have formed the entire ethos of the society. It would be a mistake to expect from a rural, oral literature, guiding principles of life in modern, urban, national and international conditions. No doubt, the literature is rich enough to continue to speak in all its moral and poetic power. But it cannot yield modern intellectual perspectives, nor be a source of answers to contemporary perplexities. Perhaps this realisation is a gain rather than a loss. For it has the potential to free the literature from chauvinist uses, as a yardstick of orthodoxy – and so, by restoring it as literature, restore its true dignity.

These observations, however, fall outside the scope of the present work. The literature of a community is one thing, the community's use (and changing uses) of it, another. It is the business of literary appreciation to study the former; the latter is the subject of historical sociology. Our concern here is with the former. I have found it necessary to include this Introduction only by way of a background. Were the background widely known, the Introduction would have been redundant. As it is, it has been supplied with some reluctance, lest the issues it raises overshadow, rather than illuminate, the poetry, which should be the prime focus, after all, of all those who care for it.

Before closing, I should like to outline the principles and the procedure I have followed in translating the hymns into English.

VIII

Despite the brave attempt of Nabokov, the novelist, to defend the 'servile path', his name for the literal translation of a poem, we have by now seen enough literal translations to know that there is no such thing. Nevertheless, we can see that what are intended as literal translations are different, as a class, from what are presented as poetic re-creations. We must conclude, then, that there is something distinct which is being assumed or intended, and carried out, in the name of a literal translation. So we must ask what this is.

Inevitably, what are intended as literal translations of poetry turn out to be, by and large, prose translations. This cannot be helped, as it is very seldom, if ever, that rhythms, rhymes, assonances, puns and alliterations, so essential to poetry, can be transformed from one language to another. What is called 'literal' translation renounces any effort not only to reproduce, but even to suggest these characteristics. It rushes, instead, to lay out the meaning. (Or perhaps we might say 'lay down', because such meanings are more often than not limp, prostrate, enfeebled).

What, then, defines this 'meaning'? It is clear that those who aim at a 'literal' translation believe – mostly unconsciously – that poetry makes statements which may be made as well in prose; and that the poetic part is but a decoration. One may love the verbal ornaments with all one's heart, but this approach betrays the assumption that the being of the poem, like the being of a person, will survive a stripping away of the ornament. Anyone who knows anything about poetry knows that this is not the case.

Or if this is too strongly put, we may wish to think of the survival of a thing after the decoration has been done away with. We may think of a room, for instance, after all its paintings, its wallpaper, its curtains have been removed, and say that the room still survives. But in what sense is this 'the room'? It is certainly that in a sense recognisable to the builder carrying a measuring-tape; but it is not a room of one's own, the room which once enclosed one, and in which one lived, felt, and dreamt. Even this example has its drawbacks, however. For there is no such thing as the bare bones of a poem.

What is called the literal translation of a poem is faithful to the original only by virtue of not being faithless. One thinks here of a chaste partner in a dull, sapless marriage, faithful by virtue of a principled refusal to stray. It is more a matter of *keeping faith* – something admirable in itself, but quite devoid of the depth of fervour possible in real, active faithfulness. This is the most one could say (and perhaps it has the merit of exactness as well) in favour of literal translation of poetry.

Essentially, literal translation proceeds by fixing on each word at a time, substituting for each word in the original, its 'equivalent' in the language of translation. But words are neither minimal nor maximal units of meaning. In any case, the permissible order of words in one language may not be so in another. Therefore, literal translation is, strictly literally, impossible.

The opposite extreme to a literal translation is a re-creation. Re-creation must be distinguished from new creation. The latter is not translation at all: it uses the original as a foil from which to take off, to write one's own poem. It is only rarely that this is forgivable, and that too only because the result is brilliant. For, genius, as Shakespeare's villains prove, excuses vice. Edward Fitzgerald's 'rendering' of Umar Khayyam comes to mind. In the great majority of cases, however, such undertakings are indecent. They show disrespect for the original work, and a corresponding admiration for the 'translator's' ego. It is one thing to have one's own fancies; another thing to make them stifle and deform another (and as it often happens, far superior) literary voice. Of such 'translations', examples are deplorably legion.

Re-creation departs from the original in this way: it substitutes another text for the original on the basis of the conviction that this is how the authors would have said their piece if they had lived in our time and place instead of theirs; and had they spoken in the language of translation, rather than of the original. It is its own brand of faithfulness, and demands its own scruples. But it is a faithfulness to the soul, to the exclusion of the body. It ought to be tried only when one's own gifts are not meagre, and when one is sure that one knows the soul in question.

Despite my predilection, for better or worse, for this type of translation, I have firmly resisted the temptation to attempt it here. I have sought to remain faithful to the body and soul of the original. As far as I know, I have not tried to 'improve' the effect in English by amending or adding to the text, even when the result, besides adding to poetic felicity in English, might have been true to the spirit of the original.

This has been so for several reasons. As already stated, these hymns are part of the living tradition of a community, and as such deserve a meticulous respect, a conservative faithfulness, even in the face of the knowledge that to have been innovative at so many individual points would clearly have led to better results in English.

Secondly, the poetry is hardly known. The first and foremost need, therefore, is to present it, not to work on it.

Thirdly, re-creation has its uses in the case of poetry which has complexities and ambiguities in the original. Baudelair's Parisian sophistication, his complex combination of hearty decadence and persistent, if agnostic, search for redemption, is a prime example. But the Ginans, with their devotional temper, their didactic impulse, their moral and doctrinal certitudes, are poetically as far as they can be not only from the literature of urban sophistication, but also from oral, legendary epics (like Homer's). They are much more straightforward. To a large degree, their power lies in their straightforwardness. As such, they demand straightforward translation.

But, for all the reasons stated above, 'straightforward' does not mean 'literal'. I must now show why this is so, and what type of challenge the Ginans pose for the would-be translator.

As a relatively uncomplicated example, consider the following satirical passage about a fraudulent master (*guru*) and his disciple:

How will they cross ashore –
The master
    with a sack on his head,
The pupil
    with a load on his head.
Both of them
    seated in a metal boat?

The original may be transliterated as follows:

Gurke sirto gāthḍi
Ane sevak sir bhār
Lohā nāv māhe besiye
To kem kari utariye pārre

A word-for-word translation would be as follows:

Master on head (to) sack.
And servant head load.
Iron boat inside [were to] sit,
Then how doing [should we] reach shore (re).

Straightaway, a number of grammatical features spring to our attention. The passage dispenses with the copula ('is') in both statements (lines 1 and 2). The genitive relation is conveyed by the postposition *ke* (which, incidentally, is a feature, not of Gujarati, but of Hindustani). *Besiye* and *utariye* are verbal forms in the subjunctive mood (which English does not mark through a suffix). They are inflected here in the first person plural, which the language allows as a means to an impersonal general statement (much like the non-specific use of 'you' in English, or of the impersonal 'one'; we might also think of the French *on*,

41

which in familiar usage amounts to 'we'). In idiomatic Gujarati it is permissible to use forms associated with 'we' to convey the sense marked by 'one'. This may have something to do with the fact that Gujarati distinguishes between an inclusive and non-inclusive pronoun in the second person plural – *āpṇe* vs. *ame*.

We should similarly note differences in acceptable word order in the two languages. Especially troublesome to a translator is the necessity in English of articles (*a, an, the*). Because these are not similarly mandatory in Gujarati, it sometimes allows greater terseness of diction. A specific feature in this particular instance are the particles *to* and *re*. *To* is often a conjunction meaning 'then', 'so', or 'for', but can also function as a particle, as it does here (line 1). The particle *re* at the end of line 4 is required musically. Such particles occur frequently in the Ginans. Along with vocatives and interjections, they are usually untranslatable. Yet they often contribute to the tone and mood, which ideally a translation must at least intimate.

Obviously, a simple word by word (and particle by particle) translation would be impossible. However, it would be perfectly possible to translate as much of it as can be done along these lines, with such changes in word order as are required in English, and with the necessary addition of copulae, auxiliary verbs, articles, etc. But then an essential feature is lost. The *melodic form* of the piece plays as large a part as (if not larger than) the syntax, in producing the rhetorical and emotional effect. The first two lines, which are complete statements, each fall to a pause after a series of parallel descents from high notes. The third line, which is a conditional clause, starts low, moves (or should move) at a slower tempo, and ends on a suspended note, awaiting the punch-line. The last line (the main clause of this sentence) begins by continuing at the lower level and then rises swiftly, reaching a crescendo. In good singing, it is essential that as the crescendo is reached, the volume must also be amplified. It is clear, then, that this is where the rhetorical climax is situated.

Had the order of lines been reproduced in the translation however, one would have risked a slackening of this rhetorical tautness. This would have been caused in part by a loss of the parallelism to be found in the original, where each of the first three lines begins with a noun or noun phrase ('Master', 'Servant', 'Iron boat'). To retain the two first lines as complete sentences would have led to a prosaic result – e.g. 'The master has a sack on his head'. An obviously better rendition would have been to start with a prepositional phrase – e.g. 'On the master's head, a sack'. But either way, in the third line we would have been obliged to start with a conditional clause, e.g. 'if we sit in an iron boat...', which is utterly unpoetic. The parallelism, which is an important contributor in the original to the sense of an argument under way, making us want it to conclude, would have been undone. And so would the unity of the stanza, which would have been sacrificed in favour of serial (rather than cumulative) sentences.

Bearing these qualities of the original in mind, and above all, with an ear to its melodic pattern, I have opted to reproduce it into a single syntactic piece. The translation opens with the question which in the original occupies the fourth line of the quatrain. Grammatically, the question makes up the whole passage, with the statements being dovetailed into it in the form of noun clauses in apposition to 'they'. This is a way of em-phasising the question, which also receives emphasis in the original. There, however, emphasis is ensured through the pre-ceding lines leading up to it. Here it is secured through the framing effect. Such re-ordering becomes necessary due to the different attributes of the languages concerned and above all, due to the shift from a singing text to a non-singing one.

Besides the 'framing' effect, I have also tried to reproduce a measure of parallelism. I have tried to ensure this through symmetry in the 'inbuilt' clauses, each of them divided into a noun or noun phrase followed by a qualifying prepositional phrase in the first two instances and a participial-adjectival one in the last. For whatever it is worth, such pattern calls for a corresponding arrangement of lines, so that the syntactic effect is reinforced by a visual and graphic impression. No purpose would have been served here by rendering the four lines in the original into four in English, in a misguided conformism. It seldom works, and I have not bothered to try. For, slavishness is not faithfulness.

The drawback of 'straightforward' translation is that it starts with words, then turns them into a sentence by making such amendments as are required by the second language, such as inserting articles, connectives, etc., reversing word-order as necessary (thus Gujarati 'Here noise much is' will have to be rendered as 'There is much noise here'). The point to be noted is twofold. First, the translation is word by word. Secondly, almost instinctively the words are ordered and added to, to satisfy the grammatical requirements of English. The fact that this second process does not receive full, conscious attention means that the shifts in meaning and effect which are due to word-order and grammatical, and for that matter, phonological features, such as intonation, accent, etc., go unnoticed. What results is at best a dilution, worse still, distortion, and at worst, destruction, of the original sense.

One conclusion which follows from all this is that a translator must not take a word, but an entire statement – a unit rather than an element – as the item to be translated. It is the relations between terms – their interplay, the parallels and the contrasts – which unfold the sense, not the discrete meaning of each term. In the passage cited above, it is this principle which has led me, in translation, to form three parallel phrases (each a noun – or pronoun cluster – plus a qualifying phrase) and to frame them into an overarching question. Gujarati does not allow such a structure without awkwardness. However, the four 'start-stop' clauses in the original cohere as a unity, by virtue of the quatrain form as well as the melody. To reproduce the stanza as a quatrain and forego the possibility of rhythm might serve a purpose for scholars; but it is poetically unforgivable. And the melody is, of course, irreproducible. In such conditions, a translator might want to 'x-ray' the piece for the rhythmic anatomy best suited, as it were, to its semantic physiology. He must then find a rhythmic-semantic analogue in English. This is what I have tried to do.

Rhythm is the principal reason why the lines in an original verse or stanza hardly ever come out in the same number in my translation. I do not see why a couplet in the original should come out as a couplet in the second language if it fails to serve the combined interests of rhythm, grammar, meaning and those elusive but important qualities: tone and feeling. There are, of course, creditable instances of such achievement in the world of poetic translations. But I, at least, have found it impossible to do likewise with the Ginans, nor am persuaded that it is important to do so. (Where such a symmetry has been achieved, it is a coincidence; but so unpersuaded am I of its importance that I cannot call it a happy coincidence – though it is not, of course, an unhappy one).

In general, English, for reasons of grammatical constraints such as the need for articles, varying prepositions, auxiliary verbs, etc., is more dilatory than the language of the Ginans. For this reason, a single line in the original often comes out as several lines in the translation (when a long line would have sacrificed the qualities that have just been emphasised). Again, for these reasons, I have sometimes found it desirable to rework the order of lines or verses in the translation, and also to run verses or stanzas together. I have always done so, however, with the principles of faithfulness to the *effect* of the original in mind (bearing in mind, again, the difference between faithfulness and slavishness).

Feeling and tone are part of that all-important, if hazily defined thing called 'atmosphere'. The atmospheric tone of the Ginans is colloquial, vigorous, didactic, scolding, combative, plaintive, sublime, piercingly beseeching, melancholically contemplative. It is never formally solemn. For this reason, I have not even been tempted by archaisms of the sort that one sometimes sees in well-meaning but infelicitous translations – such as 'behold' for 'see', and 'thou' for 'you'. Archaisms were not of course as such in 'archaic' times – witness the use of 'thou' in Middle English and early modern English, up to the 17th century. (It was its intimate connotations which led to the use of 'thou' for God – ironically it has now the opposite connotation – and to other sundry applications, e.g. as a form of mutual address, at one time, among Quakers, reflecting their egalitarian convictions). When an expression does become archaic, its use may be due to a deliberate intention to evoke an archaic atmosphere; or to an unconscious feeling of linguistic distance; or to give the text a formal, socially and culturally elevated (perhaps scriptural) status. In the case of the Ginans, archaisms betray, I believe, either the unconscious influence of a modern translator's inevitable distance from the language of the original, or a formal, liturgical reverence for the text. As for the first, it must not be forgotten that considered in its time and place, the language of the Ginans is tellingly colloquial, intimate, informal. As for the second, it is, I believe, of the utmost importance to distinguish the Ginans from the way they are organised and used in subsequent history (or phases of that history) in a communal context. I have therefore used archaisms only where the original idiom, or something about the phrasing, justifies such usage.

In particular, I have no use for ideological advocacy. It is the religious experience present in the Ginans, not religious enthusiasm on their behalf, which gives the poetry its interest and its power.

45

There can be little doubt that the Ginan-literature is anything but ill-served by misguided (if well-meaning) zeal on its behalf. Those who are under the direct, natural spell of its poetry will be moved, without artificial encouragement, to *sing* it – that is, to give voice to it, in the head and heart, and on the lips. Those, by contrast, who sing *about* the Ginans, and fight battles on their behalf, are in a state of mind wholly different from authentic appreciation of the literature. For true appreciation subordinates all attention to the literature itself. It claims exclusive focus, and neither requires, nor allows for partisanship on its behalf. Partisanship turns the literature into a fetish, a rallying-cry for agendas and anxieties external to the poetry. One may appreciate the literature in its integrity, for what it is. Or one may be obsessed with defining – and guarding – the correct ('orthodox') place for it in a community's hierarchy of doctrines and practices. In the latter circumstance, the work has lost its character as literature, and acquired status, instead, as the centrepiece in an ideology. Ideology spells the death of literature. The type of mind necessary for each of these pursuits is antithetical to the type required by the other. All *definitions* of the Ginans – e.g. as 'scripture' (criticised above), or as 'liturgy' – are external, hence irrelevant, to the poetry. So are the ritual labels given to them and the categories into which they are divided according to their alleged – usually circumstantial – ritual purposes. All these at best use the literature, and at worse, abuse it while intending to honour it. Neither benign use, nor unintended abuse, adds a jot to literary appreciation.

We have said little as yet while on the subject of translation, about the lexicon, the vocabulary. In the passage, quoted above, 'servant' had to be rendered as 'pupil' because the *gur(u)* actually means 'teacher'. The reason the text says 'servant' is because traditionally the pupil (or apprentice) is expected to *serve* the teacher, attending on every need of his, and doing his bidding ungrudgingly, indeed eagerly. 'Teacher' in English does not of course have any of these meanings. 'Master' is a happy way of uniting the two meanings. But 'servant' would have missed out on the idea of apprenticeship. Hence 'pupil', which has the merit of stressing juniority, but suggests the aspect of subservience rather faintly, whereas *sevak* proclaims it.

These incompatibilities in meaning obviously take us beyond language and into the domain of culture. At times, such cultural or philosophical untranslatibility may involve a concept with an important place in the universe of ideas carried in the poetry. A prime example is *man*. Neither 'mind' nor 'heart' are suitable translations, as *man* includes elements of both, occupying a space of meaning between them as it were, with the additional suggestion of unruliness, and a moral obligation to suppress or discipline its capricious quality. I have translated it as 'mind' or 'heart' depending on the context, but almost always with residual dissatisfaction. Occasionally, 'ego' has proved useful. It has the advantage of inviting the intended moral reaction. But, besides its Latinate aloofness, it is more a concept rather than (except in some interpretations of Freudian psychoanalysis) the name for an organ (or quasi-organ). By contrast, 'mind' and 'heart', while having conceptual or metaphoric properties, have organic counterparts.

In sum, then, vocabulary, grammar, syntax, semantics, all need to be borne in mind. It is important to remember that poetry expresses not only idea, but also feeling; and not only what is stated, but also what is evoked. Above all, one cannot reiterate too often that the melody plays a significant part in creating and modulating the meaning of the Ginans.

In the traditional style of singing the Ginans (now regrettably rare) there is a great deal of spontaneity and improvisation. Certain lines are repeated, and sometimes, the singer might add extra, impromptu repetitions. Every repetition allows a different word to be emphasised. And change of tempo contributes to this, allowing a group of words to be passed over quickly where in the preceding utterance each might have been stressed separately, and vice versa.

There was a time when, in the singing of the longer works, one sometimes heard the alternation of a speaking or narrative with a singing tone. (The effect of this has a partial analogue in the alternation of recitative and aria in European opera). Rather despairingly conscious of all this, I have sometimes made a helpless gesture as it were at the melody, through repetition, spacing or other such devices.

In any event, I have not translated any hymns here except the ones with whose tunes I am personally familiar and which I could hear in my mind.

Every stanza of every Ginan ends with a refrain in the original. This ties up the musical rhythm. In a purely verbal text however, it would destroy, rather than help the rhythm, to repeat the refrain every time. So, I have preferred to repeat or intersperse the refrain a few times, in selected places. For the same reason, I have not repeated vocatives (like 'O brother!'), and have preferred to omit the standard (semantically void) interjection, *eji*. For, translation, to start with, is an act of insolence; to burden it with the prosaic would have been to compound the impudence.

After all this preamble, one stark fact stares one in the face. I am only too acutely conscious of how pale and weak the English renditions are in comparison to the haunting, uplifting, hypnotic, musical wealth of the original. Mine is the indistinction of a messenger attempting in vain to recapitulate a message originally heard live. In relation to the original, the translation is an anaemic facsimile. If I have decided to let it see the light of day, it is in the belief, justified or not, that an anaemic facsimile is better service to those who have an interest in this literature, but cannot read the original, than none at all.

Notes

1 The Khojahs are to be distinguished from their sister Indian Ismaili community (of the Musta'li rather than Nizari branch) known as the Bohras. To avoid burdening the text, the term 'Nizari' is not repeated from here on in references to the Ismailis, it being understood that the Ginans belong to this branch of the Ismailis.
   On the Imamshahis, see W. Ivanow, 'The Sect of Imam Shah in Gujrat', *Journal of the Bombay Branch of the Royal Asiatic Society*, New Series 12 (1936), pp. 19–70. See also Dominique Sila Khan and Zawahir Moir, 'Coexistence and Communalism: The Shrine of Pirana in Gujarat', *South Asia*, Vol. XXII, Special Issue (1999), pp. 135–154.

2 For works of critical scholarship on the Ginans to date see the selected bibliography.

3 The tradition on Satgur Nur is given in *Mahān Ismaili Sant Pir Hasan Kabirdin ane Bijā Sattādhāri Piro Rachit Ginānono Sangrah 3* (Bombay, [undated]), p. 8; and in Alimohamed Chunara, *Nuram Mobin athvā Allāhni Pavitra Rasi* (Bombay, 1961), pp. 207–208, where he appears under the name of Pir Saiyad Nurdin. See also W. Ivanow, 'Satpanth', in *Collectanea*, ed. W. Ivanow (Leiden, 1948), pp. 10–11; and Azim Nanji, *The Nizārī Ismāʿīlī Tradition in the Indo-Pakistan Subcontinent* (Delmar, 1978), pp. 50–53 and 57–61.

4 An outline of Pir Shams' life, as transmitted in the Khoja tradition, is given in *Mahān Ismaili Sant Pir Shams Rachit Ginānono Sangrah 2* (Bombay, 1952), pp. 4–9. See also Chunara, *Nuram Mobin*, pp. 311–319; Ivanow, 'Satpanth', pp. 11–16; and Nanji, *Nizārī Ismāʿīlī Tradition*, pp. 53–57 and 61–69. Tazim Kassam reviews all these stories and traditions concerning the figure of Pir

Introduction

Shams, subjecting his various proposed identities to critical examination, and offering her own tentative conclusions about his identity in her work, *Songs of Wisdom and Circles of Dance: Hymns of the Satpanth Ismāʿīlī Muslim Saint, Pīr Shams* (Albany, 1995), pp. 75–116. A similar exercise, leading to her own tentative conclusions, has been carried out by Zawahir Moir, 'The Life and Legends of Pir Shams as Reflected in the Ismaili Ginans: A Critical Review', in *Constructions Hagiographiques dans le Monde Indien: Entre Mythe et Histoire*, ed. Francoise Mallison (Paris, 2001), pp. 365–384.

5   See Nanji, *Nizārī Ismāʿīlī Tradition*, p. 66.

6   On traditions concerning Pir Sadardin, see the sketch of his life introducing the collection of his Ginans, *Mahān Ismaili Sant Pir Sadardin Rachit Ginānono Sangrah I* (Bombay, 1952), pp. 6–11; and Chunara, *Nuram Mobin*, pp. 324–325. See also Ivanow, 'Satpanth', pp. 16–17, and Nanji, *Nizārī Ismāʿīlī Tradition*, pp. 72–77.

7   For Pir Hasan Kabirdin, see the sketch of his life preceding the collection of his Ginans, *Mahān Ismaili Sant Pir Hasan Kabirdin*, pp. 5–7; and Chunara, *Nuram Mobin*, pp. 325–327. For a critical discussion of dates, see Nanji, *Nizārī Ismāʿīlī Tradition*, pp. 77–79. The mention of Hasan Kabirdin as a Suhrawardi Pir is to be found in John A. Subhan, *Sufism: Its Saints and Shrines* (Lucknow, 1960), p. 359.

8   See Chunara, *Nuram Mobin*, pp. 337–338. See also Nanji, *Nizārī Ismāʿīlī Tradition*, pp. 78–81.

9   The story of Imamshah as preserved in Indian Ismaili tradition is given in Chunara, *Nuram Mobin*, pp. 333–334 (where it is recorded without judgement about the responsibility for the split) and in *Mahān Ismaili Dharmaprachārak Saiyad Imamshah ane Bijā Dharmaprachārak Saiyado Rachit Ginānono Sangrah 4* (Bombay, 1954), pp. 3–5. Shafique Virani, in his M.A. thesis, *The Voice of Truth: Life and Works of Sayyid Nūr Muḥammad Shāh, a 15ᵗʰ/16ᵗʰ Century Ismāʿīlī Mystic* (McGill University, 1995), maintains that Nurmohamed Shah was not responsible for the split. It is neither possible nor necessary for me to try to arbitrate between these differing historical arguments, which at any rate involve, to say the least, a degree of speculation.

10 See Nanji, *Nizārī Ismāʿīlī Tradition*, p. 3 and 25; Christopher Shackle and Zawahir Moir, *Ismaili Hymns from South Asia: An Introduction to the Ginans* (Richmond, 2000); pp. 9–10; Kassam, *Songs of Wisdom*, pp. 27–34.

11 See Chunara, *Nuram Mobin*, pp. 328–330, and also the individual references below.

12 The lives and traditions of these figures are given in *Mahān Ismaili Dharmaprachārak Saiyad Imamshah*, pp. 3–10; see also Chunara, *Nuram Mobin*, pp. 387–389. Additional, interesting light on Imam Begum's life and personality has been added by Zawahir Moir, 'Bībī Imām Begam and the End of the Ismaili Ginānic Tradition', in *Studies in Early Modern Indo-Aryan Languages, Literature and Culture*, ed. Alan W. Entwistle et al (New Delhi, 1999), pp. 249–265, though there are still many gaps in information about her which await further research.

13 See Nanji, *Nizārī Ismāʿīlī Tradition*, p. 10.

14 Ali Asani, 'The Khojkī Script: A Legacy of Ismāʿīlī Islam in the Indo-Pakistan Subcontinent', *Journal of the American Oriental Society*, 107, 3 (1987), p. 440.

15 See Nanji, *Nizārī Ismāʿīlī Tradition*, p. 10; Shackle & Moir, *Ismaili Hymns*, pp. 16–17.

16 The most determined treatment and classification of Ginans according to themes (seen as a 'belief system') is to be found in Shackle and Moir, *Ismaili Hymns*, pp. 23–24, and 62–141; see also Ali Asani, 'The Ginān Literature of the Ismailis of Indo-Pakistan: Its Origins, Characteristics and Themes', in *Devotion Divine: Bhakti Traditions from the Regions of India*, ed. D. Eck and F. Mallison (Groningen-Paris, 1991), p. 14. This approach has been questioned, and rightly so, by Tazim Kassam, *Songs of Wisdom*, pp. 157–158, but the objection needs to be theoretically fortified. The questions that need to be asked in this respect may be put quite simply. Where does the intellectual frame of classification come from? Is it prompted by the literature itself, or by an external frame of reference? If it is the latter, does it illuminate the literature itself, or subordinate it to extrinsically inspired interpretation?

17 Ali Asani's interesting distinction between the concepts of authority and authorship is a step in the right direction; see his 'The Isma'ili *Ginān*: Reflections on Authority and Authorship', in *Mediaeval Isma'ili History and Thought*, ed. Farhad Daftary (Cambridge, 1996), pp. 265–280.

18 Tazim Kassam is the first to have pointed out and criticised this tendency (see *Songs of Wisdom*, pp. 9–26). What I say here on this point is in part a reiteration, and in part a theoretical elaboration, of her own position on this matter.

19 Ivanow, 'Satpanth', pp. 3–4, 17, and passim.

20 The ultimately apologetic explanation of the content of the Ginan-literature as a product of a conscious strategy of conversion is a standard thesis, first put forward (in critical scholarship) by Ivanow and thereafter taken for granted and repeated by subsequent scholars. Again, credit for pointing out the deficiencies in this attribution of a 'calculating' or expedient mentality in the composition of the Ginans is due to Tazim Kassam (*Songs of Wisdom*, pp. 23–26 and 37–38). One does not have to agree with Kassam's insistence on a distinction between 'religious' and 'sociopolitical' factors in the emergence of Satpanth to endorse her reservations about the explanation of Ginanic content in terms of a conversion strategy – reservations which are sustainable independently of the other thesis. Kassam touches on an important argument when she says that the strategic explanation 'divests the tradition of its religious authenticity' (p. 25). I would take this point further, and with the aid simply of a *literary* truth. There is all the difference in the world between good literature and propaganda. The latter is by definition 'strategic'; the former reflects a sensibility organically rooted in the culture in question. That the Ginans have literary merits is, I think, not in doubt.

21 Ivanow, 'Sect of Imam Shah', p. 41.

22 This point too was first made by Tazim Kassam (see *Songs of Wisdom*, pp. 14–15 and pp. 19–26), where she rightly criticises periodisation in terms of 'pre-Fatimid', 'Fatimid' and 'post-Fatimid' phases; and p. 38, where she rejects, as I do, the interpretation of Indian Ismailism as a mere 'translation' of its Nizari counterpart. In this and the other observations cited above, Kassam's work marks a definite advance in analytic sophistication beyond her predecessors. This does not mean, however, that I agree with all aspects of her work. To begin with, there are the differences arising from my philosophical and literary points of view – differences which will be evident upon comparative examination, and therefore do not need to be laboured. More specifically, her determined belief in the political as opposed to

religious origins of *Satpanth* leads her to build too big an edifice on too slender a scaffolding (of evidence). In the process, she ends up attributing to the movement the very element of calculation and strategic expediency which she otherwise rightly deplores. (This suggestion of conscious and expedient invention is best illustrated in Kassam's remark that 'the Isma'ilis periodically attached and detached the symbolic and ritual forms of religious life from inner, religious realities as they saw fit' – *Songs of Wisdom*, pp. 71–72. One wonders, however, whether any tradition of enduring religious – and indeed literary – substance can be founded on an expedient or calculating basis alone). All in all, the kind of large-scale historical explanation that Kassam has undertaken requires not only far more historical evidence, but also a much stronger philosophical underpinning than is provided for in her work. Similarly, in her definition of the *place* of the Ginans in the Indian Ismaili community, she seems to me to neglect the varying appropriations of the literature (as with all literature carried in a community) at different times and in different contexts. None of this, however, detracts from the value and sophistication of her contribution, which puts it in a different category from many of the earlier studies.

23 Only two Ginans, to my knowledge, make it their object to provide dates and stories about Imams and Pirs. These are clearly distinguishable from passing allusions in other Ginans which are subsumed in other modes of discourse – such as parables, mythical narratives, and moral didactics. Obviously, the purpose of these other forms of discourse is not to provide empirical, historical information. As for the two Ginans which appear to aim at (among other things) the communication of historical information – namely, *Satveni Motī* and *Satvenini Vel*, discussed above, both being attributed, incidentally, to Imamshah's son, Nurmohamed Shah, they do not do so in an internally consistent or historically foolproof way.

24 The occurrence of the idea of the *nikalaṅki avatār* among specific groups in the Subcontinent is discussed by Dominique-Sila Khan in 'The Coming of Nikalank Avatar: A Messianic Theme in Some Sectarian Traditions of North-Western India', *Journal of Indian Philosophy* 25 (1997), pp. 401–426.

25 Henry Corbin, *Creative Imagination in the Sufism of Ibn 'Arabi* (Princeton, 1969), pp. 124–135, 195–200 and 265–267.

26 Paul Riceour, *Freud and Philosophy: An Essay on Interpretation*, tr. Denis Savage (New Haven, 1970), p. 525.

27 Asim, Roy, *The Islamic Syncretistic Tradition in Bengal* (Princeton, 1983), p. 95.

28 Asim, Roy, *Islam in South Asia* (New Delhi, 1996), p. 104. The incarnations, in Vaisnavite mythology are: fish, tortoise, boar, man-lion, dwarf, axe-man, (*parsurām* or *farsirām*) Rama, Krishna and Buddha (the scheme has slight local variations).

29 See Roy, *Islamic Syncretistic Tradition*, pp. 136–140.

30 Ibid., p. 91.

31 Ibid., p. 144.

32 Roy, *Islam in South Asia*, pp. 33–34.

33 On the relationship between these two traditions see, for example, Françoise Mallison, 'Muslim Devotional Literature in Gujarati: Islam and Bhakti', in *Devotional Literature in South Asia: Current Research, 1985–1988*, ed. R. S. McGregor (Cambridge, 1992), pp. 89–100.

34 See Richard M. Eaton, *Sufis of Bijapur, 1300–1700: Social Roles of Sufis in Medieval India* (Princeton, 1978), p. 151.

35 Roy, *Islamic Syncretistic Tradition*, p. 159.

36 Quoted in Lajwanti Rama Krishna, *Panjabi Sufi Poets, A.D. 1460–1900* (Calcutta-London, 1938), p. xviii and pp. 33–37.

37 Roy, *Islam in South Asia*, p.29.

38 Ibid., p. 104.

39 Roy, *Islamic Syncretistic Tradition*, pp. 161–162.

40 Ibid., p. 161.

41 See Sarah F. D. Ansari, *Sufi Saints and State Power: The Pirs of Sind, 1843–1947* (Cambridge, 1992), p. 23.

42 Ibid., p. 160.

43 For resemblances between Kabir's poetry and the Ginans, see the translations in Charlotte Vaudeville, *Kabir* (Oxford, 1974) Vol. 1, pp. 225 (no.32e), 227 (40c), 229 (6a), 233 (27b), 239 (59d), 238 (55e), 239 (61f), 240 (67f), 246 (6e), 248 (14c), 257 (1d), etc., and especially, pp. 249 (19d) and 251 (33e).

44 Ali Asani has commented on the mixture of materials in the Harvard collection in his Introduction to *The Harvard Collection of Ismaili Literature in Indic Languages: A Descriptive Catalog and Finding Aid* (Boston, 1992). Remarks tantamount to the attribution of a scriptural status to the Ginans – remarks which are historically questionable, as I suggest above, besides being unrepresentative of the entirety of the community today – are recorded in Asani, 'The Ismaili *Gināns* as Devotional Literature', in *Devotional Literature in South Asia: Current Research, 1985–1988*, ed. R. S. McGregor (Cambridge, 1992), p. 103.

45 See Roy, *Islam in South Asia*, pp. 20–23.

46 As cited by Imtiaz Ahmad, 'Exclusivity and Assimilation in Indian Islam', in Attar Singh, *Socio-Cultural Impact of Islam on India* (Chandigrah, 1976), p. 99.

47 Roy, *Islam in South Asia*, p. 14.

48 Richard Eaton, *Essays on Islam and Indian History* (New Delhi, 2000), p. 46. The emphasis is mine.

49 Ahmad, 'Exclusivity and Assimilation', p. 94.

50 Ibid., p. 95.

51 Ibid., pp. 96–97.

52 Ronald Robertson, *The Sociological Interpretation of Religion* (Oxford, 1970), p. 104.

53 Derryl N. MacLean, *Religion and Society in Arab Sind* (Leiden, 1989), p. 35.

Interpretative Essay

I

One of Pir Shams' Ginans opens with the following sequence of verses:

> In my heart He lives, Allah
> The Creator, He who fashioned
> Nature's eternal scheme.
>
> Say, O *mullāh*! Say,
> O *qāzi*! Who was it
> Who made this universe?
>
> From this dust
> Was this entire world made.
> Who shall we say
> In all this
> Is the Hindu? And the Musalman?
>
> The Hindu is he who proceeds
> To the sixty-eight shrines.
> The Musalman, he who proceeds
> To the mosque.

A number of characteristic features of Ginan-literature are succinctly present in these verses. The Ginan begins with an exaltation of the human 'heart'. Although the grammatical subject of the first verse in the original is 'Allah', 'heart' forms the *theme* of the sentence. The opening line declares, straightaway, the *vastness* of the heart. For it is the home of God. A home which can accommodate such an all-exalted tenant is no mean place. As if to emphasise this point, the person of 'Allah' is further described through His attributes. He is the 'Creator', 'He who fashioned/Nature's eternal scheme'. These epithets magnify 'Allah', all the more so as to emphasise the immensity of the heart, which is where He lives.

The second verse poses a question. Both the question, and the identity of those to which it is addressed, are significant. The *mullāh* and the *qāzi* (from Arabic *qāḍi*) are clerics, scholars, representatives of 'official', orthodox Islam. There is an audible note of mockery in the question. The answer is so obvious and matter-of-fact as to make the question superfluous. That it is put to these particular figures, experts in religion, adds irony to the superfluity. The effect can only be to intensify the taunting, mocking tone.

The third verse introduces a statement – we thus have a statement between two questions. The entire world, we are reminded, is made of dust. This reminder of the insubstantiality of everything in the world serves to underline the contrasting substantiality of the yet more encompassing 'heart', the seat of the Creator. Next, it hurls another question – like a gauntlet, to borrow a metaphor from another cultural context. Who in such a world are we to call a Hindu, and a Muslim?

Where the world is built of 'dust', where reality is solely the Creator's, and where He is to be found is in the inner sanctuary of the heart, what do the conventional identities of 'Hindu' and 'Muslim' matter? Whatever definition is offered, it is certain to be an anticlimax.

True to expectation, the answer which follows has a note of bathos. The Ginan deliberately chooses, in defining the difference between Hindu and Muslim, to single out their ritual peculiarities. It seems bent on a *reductio ad absurdum*, the better to highlight thereby *another* contrast, one which goes to the heart of things, and is of far greater moment than differences of creed and convention. This deeper contrast is between worship from the heart and worship of externalities. Compared with the enormous space which separates the ardent motions of the soul from mechanical gestures of convention-bound, soulless rites, the other difference, between one creed and another, one set of rituals and another, is of little account. In fact, the latter differences are only secondary. In their spiritual shallowness, they share a kinship deeper than superficial differences of creed. Conversely, the contrast between a faith of spirit, and a religion devoid of spirit, makes a world of difference even if they both belong, superficially, to a shared creed.

The next verse of the Ginan goes on to dissociate true worship, the true worshipper, and the true object of worship, from their spurious opposites. Slaves of orthodoxy, the Ginan declares, can have no possible inkling of the God whose very being is pure, aloof, impervious to the manipulations of lifeless worship.

After this work of demolition, the ground is ready for positive statement. Already, the last-cited verse marks a shift from negation to affirmation. It has two statements, of which the first denies the possibility of knowledge of God to addicts of formalism, while the second asserts His simultaneous transcendence and nearness. (He transcends the ritualism in which the orthodox believers insist on caging Him. But he is also proximate, because seated 'within'). The two verses which follow clinch the argument, and add further claims of magnificent audacity:

> Not Hindu, nor Musalman
> Knows my Lord.
> My Lord is seated
> Pure, immaculate.

> My mind
> Is my prayer-mat.
> Allah, my *qāzi*.
> My body, a mosque.

> Seated within,
> I say my *namāz*.
> What can the fool know
> Of my prayer?

The first verse juxtaposes two statements: one negative, the other positive. The first sentence has two exactly parallel negative clauses in the original. (This structure is not reproduced in my translation because of the resulting inelegance in English). Translated literally, the sentence runs: 'My Lord the Hindu does not know, the Musalman does not recognise'. There is thus a single sentence with two clauses, two subject nouns, two practically synonymous verbs, and a single object ('my Lord'). The effect is to emphasise 'my Lord', the common object in the two clauses, and also the term which heads the sentence. The near-synonymity of the verbs ('know' and 'recognise') seems to play down the difference suggested in the two subject–nouns ('Hindu' and 'Musalman'). The sense conveyed is that both, to the extent that they might be obsessed with external forms, are alike. What they share is the negative condition of 'not-knowing' (a term preferable to 'ignorance', as what is implied is not only an absence of knowledge, but an active blindness). The Lord, who is Pure Being, is above the ritual formalism of both Hinduism and Islam, neither of which, in this form of religion, can apprehend Him. Both in meaning and grammar, therefore, the affirmative emphasis falls on the Divine, which is dissociated, through these means, from all false worship. The true God is both the subject and object of the affirmation.

This chord of affirmation reverberates into the succeeding verse. It is taken up there into a series of fresh assertions, of breathtaking boldness. The living body is the very house of worship. Nothing else than the mind or ego will do as a prayer-mat. The ego, a bundle of passions which entrap it in the world, is the chief enemy which the true worshipper will seek to subjugate. The triumphant note in this image is of a piece with the rejection of formalism stated in those very lines. Finally, none else but the Creator Himself will lead the prayer. The dead rubble of formalism has now been swept aside. In its place has stepped the living person, master over his unruly passions, and fully cognizant of his bond with his Maker.

It may be interesting to look at the grammatical structure of these passages a little more closely. The negative statements in the first of the three last-quoted verses on one hand, and on the other hand, the positive statements in the second, are structurally parallel. Each has a short subject, verb and complement. However, the verbs in the second verse are implicit rather than explicit. This makes the declarations all the more terse – more forceful, because more condensed. This grammatical identity makes the contrast between them – the contrast of negative to positive – all the more stark. Moreover, each statement is self-contained, without a conjunction to link them. This gives them an absolute, categorical sense. Only the structural parallelism and the inner logic of meaning connects them. Their force, present in their brevity, is not diluted by conditional, circumstantial, or any other type of qualification.

The third of the verses quoted above rounds off the assertions. The first line makes explicit what is already implied in the foregoing propositions. It is within the body, the temple of God, in which true worship takes place. Of this type of worship, the 'fool', slave to externalities, will always be ignorant. The very nature of his 'folly', his blindness, debars him from such knowledge. By now, the Ginan has both mapped out the interior sanctuary of the heart, and shut its gates against the ignorant multitudes.

In short, a boundary has been traced. But the boundary is not denominational, not sectarian, nor ideological. It marks off truth from untruth; true speech, true action, true awareness, from their counterparts in untruth. It marks off true from false ways of being – shows up the contrast, we might say, of being and pseudo-being.

We should note, in passing, how typically 'Sufi' all this is. Many Ginans differ from Sufism, but here the similarity cannot be greater.

As anyone with informed sensitivity to poetry knows, poetic literature has its own characteristic logic. But this logic is seldom linear. Poetic argument is rarely constructed like a legal verdict or a philosophical argument. Where it is thus constructed – as in John Donne – the logic of argument does not exhaust the logic of the poetry. Ginan-literature belongs to the opposite end of the spectrum to the one marked 'learned'. It is as far away from a poetic equivalent of scholarly thought as we may care to imagine. Scholarly thought is by definition the business of an academic mind. It employs the intellect of the logician and an imagination serving that intellect. The Ginans employ the religious imagination of an oral culture, and an intellect serving that imagination. It would be foolish to expect, of such literature, the logic characteristic of scholastic prose; just as it would be foolish to expect narrative realism in a folk-tale; or the contrapuntal harmonies of a Bach keyboard piece in the evenly advancing melody of an Indian *rāga*.

If we listen to the Ginans with an ear to their poetic logic (not forgetting their musical logic too) we find, first of all, a set of polarities: heart/body, truth/untruth, inner/outer, reality/illusion, death/life. But the Ginans do not simply present these polarities. These are not static oppositions, but elements in a dynamic vision. The poetic dynamics of this vision are worthy of examination.

II

One of the standard ingredients in this dynamic is metaphor. In the Ginan which we analysed above, we saw metaphor in action. When it defines the Hindu and the Muslim by their places of worship, the reference is literal. But when it goes on to speak about the body and mind as the mosque and the prayer-mat respectively, we have of course entered the realm of metaphor. What is interesting is that the displacement, in the sphere of meaning, of the external by the internal (and of the superficial by the deeper) should in this way correspond to the replacement, in language, of literal by metaphorical reference.

If we seek further instances of the contrast between the 'outer' and the 'inner', we will come upon a passage like the following, marvellous in its pregnant simplicity:

On the housetop
Shines the light
While dark night
Reigns within.
Futile
Are the outward ablutions
When the interior grime
Stays with you all the while.

The first two statements are brief and matter-of-fact. Each has a noun or noun-phrase (light/dark night) and a preposition or prepositional phrase (on the housetop/within). In the original there are no verbs, and so again, the effect is one of trenchant, concise sharpness. Significantly, this grammatical parallelism co-exists with exactly opposite ideas: illumination on the outside, darkness inside. While at one level we perceive a resemblance, at another we hear a contradiction. This lends the lines a strong irony, giving them every push as it were, for maximal impact.

Irony is indeed the essential force of these lines. Just at this point, however, the statements beg for an argument, for poetic resolution. If the lines which follow were done away with, the effect would be clearly unsatisfactory. We would be left in somewhat of a suspense, the sense of an arrested movement. We would have a scene, but a scene without meaning. This meaning has to be existential: it must involve us – not only speak to us, but about us. And this is precisely what the remaining lines provide.

These lines declare this picture to be 'futile'. But in fact, the picture itself has changed. The passage swaps subjects half-way, substituting washing for lighting. We feel that it is the same thing being talked about, but we do not know that it is the same until we arrive at the idea of interior dirt, and with it, the implied activity of interior cleansing. Now everything is clear; we see the *point* of the picture presented to us. It speaks to us when it is no longer just a picture, but an *analogy*. Outward illumination is to inward darkness as outward cleansing is to inward dirtiness. But there is more: what can inward dirt ('grime') be? This is clearly a metaphor. We recall the universal symbolism, in the history of religion, of purity and pollution. In this symbolic scheme, the physical realities of dirt and cleanliness – to speak of these is already to interpret, for the natural elements in themselves are neither 'dirty' nor 'clean' – become ethical concepts. The passage thus takes us from one domain to another via the connecting door of metaphor. Employing a set of very simple, domestic images, it shifts the level of meaning from the physical to the ethical. Through this shift, the logic of the images becomes existential. It turns the statements not only into an argument, but an argument *involving us*. The process works simultaneously both in the text and in the reader's being. In the text, a small number of extremely simple, totally homely images are strung into an argument through a shift from literal to symbolic reference. An equivalent process is expected to occur in us (that is, if the poetry works for us – which here means working *on us*). The reader – or rather, the reciter and auditors – are asked to transform the very core of their personal existence. A metaphorisation of meaning goes hand in hand with a metamorphosis of being.

Ethical transformation involves more than an alteration. By itself, change is a mere datum. It is, as we would nowadays say, a neutral event in nature. For it to be charged with value, it must belong to something more encompassing – a 'philosophy', a world-view, in which a mode of being held up as an ideal is contrasted with a 'fallen' or corrupted mode of being. This conception lies at the heart of all religion. Hence the notions of salvation and damnation.

In the Ginans, this idea takes the accents typical of mystical, as opposed to orthodox, religion. While orthodox faith insists on correct performance, hence visible conformity to tradition, mystical religion puts the stress elsewhere – to a way of being rather than performance, inner fidelity instead of demonstrative compliance. Rather than outward, public conformity, it stresses an inward alignment with the reality behind the world. It is acutely sensitive to the difference between the real and what only masquerades as real; between true being and pseudo-being.

Many analogies are employed in the Ginans, all of them simple and mundane, to drive home the fundamental difference between the real and the unreal. Take, for instance, the following image, drawn from elementary commerce (suggesting, by the way, that the people to whom the Ginans spoke were not – at least not only – rural peasantry):

> This coin that you made,
> Of an amalgam of lead
> And coppery melt,
> Floated on the bazaar,
> Will not make it far.
>> For no hand will deign to bear
>> the coin it knows is fake.

> The genuine coin
> Is struck in the mint.
> That's the real coin.
>> Floated on the bazaar,
>> None will declare it fake.

There is no indulgence here in fine distinctions, in the equivocations so beloved of scholastic discourse – nothing remotely suggestive of the complex verbal choreography of theologians and philosophers. A thing is either true or false, genuine or counterfeit. There is no mistaking the two. The difference can be told immediately and forthrightly. There is no place for 'grey' here, only black and white. The choice is stark, and it is up to us to go for the real thing, and so gain the kingdom of the spirit, or for the fraudulent item, and so be condemned to delusion.

The metaphor of currency works on us without our being told to equate the opposing ideas of true and false to their supposedly 'symbolised' referents. No doubt, we know that there is some deeper significance to the image; we are hardly likely to think that we are being advised to be on our guard the next time we make a round of the shops. We know that we are being morally instructed, that one's spiritual state is at stake. But this is not a separate idea, 'symbolised' by a symbol. We do not think of the coin as an 'x' standing for a 'y'. Nothing detracts more from one's appreciation of the Ginan-literature than to read it, for instance, as though it were allegorical Ismaili literature in its Arabic or even Persian schools. It has no resemblance to the *ta'wil* of Fatimid texts, which is based on scriptural and textual reading, and predicates a *batin* beneath a *zahir*, both in scripture, and in the Book of Nature.

Allegorical interpretation or *ta'wil* was the joint product of Quranic exegesis and Platonic and Neoplatonic philosophy. This is not a matter merely of different literary forms, but of two entirely different organisations and conceptions of the world. In the one case, we have a state, and a ruling elite which includes, of necessity, a learned elite, charged with providing ideological underpinnings to a religio-political system. Like the political and institutional organisation it reflects, the doctrine has parts and sub-parts, logically hierarchic and inter-related; like it, it has head-concepts and subordinate concepts which branch out from them, and stand to them in a relation of logical dependence. It is only in such a milieu that 'interpretation' of texts, let alone allegorical interpretation, can arise at all.

Here, instead, we have a non-hierarchical, non-institutionalised society (albeit with its own strong traditions of authority). Its culture is non-scholastic. No doubt, it is a culture rich in ideas, but it is a richness of another sort. These ideas are *ultimately* (and not immediately) derived from scriptural and other ancillary texts. But these are not encountered and studied as texts. They pervade the atmosphere of the society. They are the spiritual bread and butter of the people, orally imbibed and transmitted, and in the process, continually adapted. It is from this atmosphere that the Ginans draw their substance, whose elements they re-deploy so as to drive home their own convictions and ideals.

Thanks to these traditions, the society had a philosophy of life of another sort than the one which we associate with formal disciplines of philosophy and theology. We are here in the realm of mythology, folk-tales, poetic and proverbial wisdom. Through these means, one thinks of the world in the binary terms of what is truly real and what is only apparent; of what is good and what is bad; hence, of what it truly behoves a man to think and do, and to avoid. And all this is conveyed through a literary mode which is expressive rather than discursive, and finds its ideas in concrete objects and situations.

Even as we follow the poem, then, we read it at various levels. We understand the straightforward difference between legal mint and counterfeit, and we simultaneously grasp its significance in our personal existence, so that when we come later in the Ginan to the words:

> The Lord has come to tell
> The true from the fake,
> As the scriptures testify.
> All too thoroughly
> Will he examine,
> Weighing, melting,
> Probing to the core,

we are not in the least surprised or thrown off by this turn of meaning. It is a perfectly smooth and logical progression. We ourselves are the coin held up for inspection. There is no allegory here, hence no call for exegesis. Strictly speaking, there are no *levels* of meaning, rather, a *depth* of meaning. Everything in our familiar world becomes a signifier of certain key themes. Here we have the overarching difference between truth and untruth, substance and shadow. In a resounding echo of prophetic discourse, we are told that at the end of times – of *our* time, our life – the Lord will put the metal of the coin, the mettle of our being – to searching examination. Whatever is authentic in it will endure; what is corrupt will perish.

This drive for truth, for authentic being, is the ruling motif of the Ginans. Speak the truth at all times, act aright, walk the way of truth, think in truth, *be* the truth – relentlessly, the Ginans press these demands on their audience. The moral vision of the Ginans goes beyond a ritual or moral code. There is, of course, a ritual and moral code here, as in all religion. Sometimes, indeed, the code stands out in a stark form, as is readily evident in some of the Ginans translated here (and still more evident in a Ginan like *So kiriyā*). The Ginans insist on ritual observance, and they take for granted that there is right and wrong behaviour. They are not, of course, a modern, liberal manifesto, allergic to 'do's and don'ts'. Their moral radicalism is of a different sort.

In the manner of so many 'radical' visionaries – of Jesus in his acidic jibes against the Pharisees, the Sufis in their scorn of orthodox formalists, Sikh *gurus* and Hindu devotional poets at odds, all of them, with legalism and ritualism – the Ginans assert that there is no act which is right, no matter how right (i.e., how *correct*) its form unless it is performed in its meaning and its truth. In this scheme, a way of acting in the world is inseparable from a way of seeing and a way of being. Similarly, the idea of 'knowledge' in the Ginans is very different from formal book-knowledge. It is far from enough to know *about* the truth. What is essential is to live it, and to know it by living it. This is *vital* knowledge. To know truly is to be one with truth. All else is vanity, and worse. To be complacent on the basis of scriptural learning, and punctilious observance of ritual codes, betrays an egotism, a vanity. It is to be vainglorious, as well as to have lived in vain. Vanity in these two senses – conceit and sterility – is vanity also in a third sense: emptiness, absence of reality. In this way, morality, meaning and being are grasped in a single vision, each element inseparable from the other.

This unrelenting focus of the Ginans on what is 'really real', as opposed to everything impermanent, all that is show and glitter, but no substance – this distinction (to speak with Plato) between appearance and reality – is hugely rich in poetic potential. It strikes an inexhaustible vein of metaphors, paradoxes, ironies and related figures of speech. Perhaps the most potent source of poetic meditation is the experience of life and death. Human life and death, and natural being and non-being, are kindred phenomena. By marrying them across, and with the polar opposites of truth and untruth, one reaps a poetic windfall, in which life in certain forms comes to be seen as death, and death, metaphorically re-interpreted, becomes a higher form of life. This cluster of ideas is rich enough to deserve close examination.

III

The following passage of the *Saloko Nāno* illustrates very well the symbolic play on life and death just mentioned:

> Everyone dies a false death
> And none dies the true way.
> He who dies
> In wisdom divine
> Has no more deaths to die.

Dying truly, the same work will go on to explain (reminding one of what the mystics say) is to kill the ego, to smash the cauldron of one's passions and desires, and so to die in life – to die to the world, to world-obsessed life.

Thus, into the contrast between this life and life after death, between death and life before and after death, there is injected the contrast between truth and untruth. Now death can be seen as supreme affirmation: when its bells toll, they announce a new life, an awakening from the sleep of illusion. Conversely, a life lived in untruth is a pseudo-life, a form of illusion, of unreality – hence, in essence, a death.

All religions are concerned with the phenomena of life and death. The finiteness of human life, subject to pitfalls from so many directions, and ultimately to death, is the very *leitmotif* of religious thought. 'O death, where is thy sting?' – so says St. Paul in the Letter to the Corinthians. This readiness to defy death, daring it to do its worst, and be conquered in the process, is a characteristically religious motif. Here the religious mind grapples with the very limits of the knowable, the outermost frontiers of rationality. By its very nature, only a mythopoetic, rather than a rationalistic mind can grasp and handle these sentiments. Religious thought and emotion feed liberally on the human experience of the brevity and vulnerability of life on earth. Acutely conscious of the threat that death poses, not only to life, but also to its meaning or purpose, religious thought seeks to conquer death through its symbolic weaponry. Indeed, at this point, non-traditional philosophies like Heidegger's (in which death imparts meaning to life) are at one with the great religious traditions.

Symbolic representations of conquest over death include the idea of resurrection and of paradise and hell (often understood literally, but as often rationalised allegorically, though both interpretations are equally mythical in the sense indicated here). These symbols are basic to the Semitic faiths. Different traditions within each of these religions, in their turn, utilise different elements from this pool of ideas. On the other hand, the eastern religions of Hinduism and Buddhism think in terms of a cycle of reincarnations to which the soul is bound so long as it does not come to be purified through virtuous conduct and self-realisation.

The doctrine of reincarnation is a very old one, as is evident in its presence in cultures across the world from Ancient Greece, Africa, through to India. It is not to be found, of course, in scriptural traditions in the Semitic languages. However, it was one of the elements in the extraordinary mix of cultural traditions in the Near East, and was thus one of the contenders in the battle of ideas which shaped the course of the Semitic civilisations. Like the doctrines of the ancient religions of Manicheanism and Zoroastrianism, the doctrine of reincarnation was treated by these religious traditions as heretical. It would be surprising, though, if the idea had been entirely eliminated. Certainly, in India it remained all-important, and not only in Hinduism. Popular Islam, including Sufism, retained it, together with a host of other significant, indigenous ideas and symbols, as shown in the Introduction.

Like Arabo-Persian Islam, Arabo-Persian Ismailism vigorously repudiated this doctrine. The Fatimid Caliph al-Mu'izz is reported to have sharply reprimanded one of his missionaries in Sind for tolerating the belief. By the time we come to the Ginans, however (which, as was argued in the Introduction, should be seen as indigenous Ismailism, by no means definitive – any more than any other forms in Ismaili history – of 'Ismailism' as such), we find this theme very much part of their texture.

Perhaps 'theme' is the wrong word. The doctrine is not canvassed or urged – it is a given, taken for granted. It is part of the atmosphere from which the literature inhales its substance. The Ginans *invoke* the doctrine; they do not *assert* it. An asserted idea is the object of thought; an invoked idea is a means, often unconscious, to some other conscious object or purpose. In any case, this doctrinal diversity, so natural in a historical perspective, appears perplexing only if one thinks in terms of a uniform 'Islam' or 'Ismailism', transcending space and time. This is one of the many instances which illustrate the paramount importance of *contextual* understanding.

To contextual reasoning, we should add the need for mythopoetic appreciation. When we treat poetry as poetry, and not as theology or philosophy, or as the expression of a creed, we no longer treat its content literally. Freed from an extraneous straining after belief, the symbol reveals its existential eloquence – its power to give speech to the conditions of human existence on earth. Interpreted as a symbol, reincarnation conveys the horror of repetition. Such is its power that it resonates with other mythical motifs, with other connotations, and from distant cultures in time and place – such as, for instance, the myth of Sisyphus. Other symbolic ideas, of course, give voice to other dimensions of human experience. The greater the number of such competing symbolic motifs, the wider the varieties of human experience comprehended through them. The more insistent an urge to nail down a hard-and-fast definition – what Matthew Arnold called 'an irritable reaching after facts' – the larger the price paid in the limitation thus imposed on human experience. We are reminded here of Coleridge's famous motto about poetry. Nowhere does it seem more pertinent than with respect to religious poetry. What is called for is a 'suspension of disbelief' – together, we might add, with a suspension of belief.

As it happens, the Ginans are eclectic rather than exclusive in this regard. They mention not only reincarnation, but also what we might call the prophetic model of life after death. Both are present without contradiction, without a straining after logical resolution. The concern to straighten out concepts in their inter-relationship is typical of the philosopher and the theologian, just as the concern to impose the 'correct' ideas and outlaw incorrect ones is typical of the religious jurist. Such concern is unknown to the prophet, essentially an announcer of good tidings and the doom to come. It is equally foreign to the religious poet, who sings in the prophet's wake. In the Ginans one is told that to know the truth, which can be done only through the true faith, is necessary for smashing, once and for all, the relentless chain of *karma*, of action and its consequences, which make the wheel of rebirth spin on and on. In this way, the idea of re-birth is invoked not to promote it as an object of belief, but to promote commitment to the true faith. The idea of myriad rounds of birth (eight hundred and forty thousand, to be exact, according to ancient Indian belief), invokes the sense of a human ordeal on a formidable scale. This foreboding is turned into a case for seeking salvation through wholehearted commitment, a surrender of body, mind and soul, to the true faith.

The other model – what we called the 'prophetic model' – with its emphasis on judgement in the hereafter by God, and of paradise and hell as alternative destinations, exists harmoniously, side by side, with the doctrine of reincarnation. In fact, the prophetic model is more pronounced, more consciously elaborated. Reincarnation occurs in a formulaic form. But the other idea is more often elaborated, and frequently in vivid, graphic terms. We are never presented with an anecdote or a descriptive account of a soul caught in the cycle of rebirth. We are only reminded, in passing, of the misery of such a fate. But the other idea, divine judgement in the hereafter on one's conduct in the world, forms the subject of the whole of a short Ginan (translated in this volume) and of many verses in numerous other hymns. Finally, there are yet other perspectives on death. There is the 'mystical' model, different from the prophetic one, in which the true end of the soul's sojourn in life is seen as union with the divine essence. Thus, several complementary or interlocking models of life and death are present.

Textbooks of religion tend to tell us what various religions *believe* about what happens after death. But if we were to look nearer home, to our experience in the here and now – we can better appreciate the existential and moral significance of notions of life beyond death. Ironically, theologies of life after death are lifeless, 'bloodless', unless given poetic flesh and blood. (The supreme poetic example is Dante). It would seem that a prime object of symbolic ideas of life after death is to make men think of life in a different perspective – as ephemeral, part of a greater whole. Likewise, the aim is to present the universe as a moral order, in which what really matters is sharply distinguished from what, in this perspective, appears trivial and insignificant.

But if all this is going to have an existential impact, the event of death must be *felt* and *imagined* – experienced, in short, to the fullest extent possible, in advance of the event.

The Ginans are a case in point. Time and again, they paint the deep gloom of the moment of death. They tell us of what death will do to a man as we know him – how suddenly it will strike; how it will reduce the comeliest of human physiques into fodder for vermin; how it will turn the most glittering spectacle of pomp and power to dust. All this is harped on again and again. This bleak vision of man has universal analogies. In the religious literature of the Near East, we will encounter it in the Psalms. In the Quran, reminders of the weakness and fragility of human life serve as a rebuke to attitudes of pride and self-sufficiency. But the Quran is also, of course, an 'activist' message. Medieval Christian culture was dominated, by contrast, with an acute consciousness of the hereafter. The situation of medieval Islam is more complex. Sufism cultivated a strong, ascetic, world-negating mentality. But the Islam of the broad juristic, mercantile and 'bourgeoisie' classes aimed at a balance between this-worldliness and God-fearing otherworldliness.

Indian culture historically embraced opposite extremes. The caste-order entailed detailed codes of conduct though these must not be confused with this-worldly concentration of moral responsibility in the individual soul characteristic of the Judaeo-Christian-Islamic traditions. Yet this very lack of inhibition allows for a free acceptance of all varieties of human experience. The result was the presence, side by side, of a voluptuous hedonism on one hand, and self-mortifying asceticism on the other.

In the Ginans, there is a palpable strain of asceticism. But much of it is *inner* asceticism – an austerity of mind and spirit, of the kind to be found in Sufism as well as in many Hindu and Buddhistic sub-traditions – together with reminders of the frailty of life. As in the Quran, in the Ginans too there are constant reminders of how man stands continually under the judgement of God. To this theme the Ginans add the concept of *maya*, the great, all-pervasive Illusion, to explain why it is that man is chronically forgetful of this fact. If only he could remember the certainty of death, and so rouse himself from his sad, oblivious sleep, and align his soul to the Truth, the Reality which is God!

This is the didactic part of the Ginans. But every now and then, a more 'poetic', expressive part comes to the fore. Thus, in the following verse, there is no express preaching. There is only a statement of fact, which does nothing to weaken its moral impact, rather enhances it:

Barren lands
　　　　get resettled.
And the impoverished
　　　　get rich again.

But consider this marvel
> of marvels:
The dead
> do not get
> to live again.

Here no doctrine, whether of reincarnation or resurrection, intrudes to soften the sheer facticity of death. No matter how precipitate one's fall from fortune, how thorough the destruction of a human settlement, there is always the prospect of a revival. But death is final. There is, of course (in the Ginans' firm belief) the life to come. But in our phenomenal experience, the fact of death, unlike all other privations, is irreversible. It is the mystery of mysteries. What does this haunting enigma teach us? The entire philosophical, doctrinal, moral framework of the Ginans will elsewhere drive home the message that everything that has to do with this life is ultimately insubstantial. Here, however, for once, a poetic statement leaves everything else in temporary suspension.

We are given three simple, parallel statements, each with different subjects but closely parallel predicates, with the third, the climax of the piece, separated from the other two by a different construction – an imperative form with an exclamatory tone – preparing us for what follows, by announcing that what we are to consider is something quite unlike the cases cited. When the climax arrives, it does not shout; it speaks quietly, hence all the more powerfully. The effect gains quiet force through its grammatical correspondence to the first two statements, save for one difference: where they each contain an affirmative verb, this last one gives us a negative. But what a force is compressed in this simple negation! How loudly does it speak in its calmness! This is where the poetry breaks forth from the level beneath the doctrine, reinforcing it, to be sure, but also appealing, not just to our capacity for belief, but to our here-and-now observation of life and death.

We are in the realm here of uncanny wonder, a realisation of the sheer contingency of the world. Western philosophy too, in its poetic moments, shared this realisation – as in the question which runs like an incantation through Heidegger's work: Why is there something rather than nothing?

It hardly needs adding that in the Ginans, the negatives of illusion, the brevity of life, and the levelling effect of death, do not produce nihilism, but are the means rather, to a positive faith. A faith of adamantine strength for having conquered the negatives, having put death (as it were) in its place. The dominant note in the Ginans is this positive emphasis on the ultimate reality, in whose presence the privations of life turn out to be powerless. They are invoked not so as to engender a sense of the absurdity of life, but to rotate one's gaze away from false glitter, and in the direction of the Real, the light of lights.

IV

So far in the course of this essay, we have made it a point to enclose the word 'mystical' in quotation marks. This is out of a wariness of such general categories. 'Typical' categories give us the illusion of mastery of a subject through the attachment of a label, and help us parcel it out into pigeon-holes. The Ginans are a complex of many elements, and no single category will do justice to them. This is especially true of a category in which the Ginans are often placed in secondary discourse about them – namely, 'devotional literature'. The term is all right insofar as it describes a genre. But it is also misleading in that it implies that the literature is essentially an outpouring of devotion. A mere glance at it will show that this is not the case. While there is abundant devotional expression, there is much else besides. If we look at the subject linguistically, for example, it is clear that devotion involves the vocative mode, the mode of address. But the Ginans embrace many linguistic forms besides the vocative. There are creation stories, eschatological accounts, fragments of ancient epic narratives. There are parables, didactic admonitions, moral comment on life in the world. There is cosmology and doctrine. There are references to the over-arching figure of the Imam. There are allusions to legendary heroes and to the great Pirs. There are reports of mystical visions and mystical ecstasy. There are descriptions of meditative technique, and a ranking of stages of enlightenment. In short, the content is truly multifarious.

(It should be added that the translations included in the present volume do not span this entire range. However, they do give a good idea of the variety. A subsequent volume will extend this sample).

One of the elements in this stock of themes is the sense of an intimate bond, a deep affinity, like that of a child and mother, between the human self and the Divine Being. Whether we call this bond 'devotional' or 'mystical' matters less than the quality of feeling it encapsulates. To see some of its nuances, it will suffice to compare the following straightforward assertion:

The Lord is present
In the heart
At every breath

which is a doctrinal statement, remarkable for its terse lucidity, with:

The towering walls,
The flowing stream beneath.
I'm a fish in the stream.
    Come, Lord, come,
    come to the rescue.

For lack of your sight,
I'm all distraught.
Beloved, come home,
    Lord, come
To this devotee
Who neglected his devotions.
Lord, show yourself,
        show
Your beauteous face.

which is part-image, part-description, part-prayer, powerful in its own way.

It will be seen that this second quote is a complex amalgam of sensibilities. A vast, unbridgeable distance separates the human self (represented as a fish) from God-on-High. Not only is the physical distance immense, represented in the lofty tower walls. There is also an absence of bridgehead between the two environments. A fish cannot quit its habitat of water, let alone scale a massive stone-wall. The morale is that the soul is in utter need of divine grace. It has no innate capacity for rising out of its natural medium and reaching the exalted heights to which it

71

aspires. The power for bringing this about lies with God. It is He who will initiate, enable, empower, redeem. No advance in this direction can be by human volition alone. For ultimately, the human self stands in need of grace, and of grace it is athirst.

Yet, does not this thirst, this longing, this ardent upward gaze, carry the seeds of its own fulfilment? The very fact that the soul (the 'fish') can envision (like the poet) the lofty heights above; the fact that it can aspire to it; that it can do so in love; that it has a voice in which to cry out to its saviour; that it can seek the divine face which, while absent, is also in some way already present (for the craving for a specific face implies a prior intimation of it) – all these facts suggest that what the soul yearns for is already deeply joined to it. A relation which at one level appears to be a relation in distance, in separation, is at another level a long-established bond. That is why the image of two totally disparate spaces and entities – water and land, fish and stone walls – can be followed by conversational overtures in the most intimate, most tender of tones. That is why the human subject can call out to the Divine Object to reveal itself in its own 'home'. If the home of the soul is also the place where God is most at home, it is because that place is already, in a sense, a home of God.

This simultaneous confession of the deepest of bonds on one hand, and on the other, of imperfection and 'fallenness' – not, to be sure, original sin in the Christian sense, but the secondary pathology of worldly illusion – is the source of the poetic power in literature of this type. If there were only a settled sense of the unity of the human and the divine, we would have a literature of celebration, not a poetic expression of longing. If there were only a sense of divine transcendence, we would have a literature of homage and worship, not a yearning filled, as here, with tender intimacy. And this pattern of meaning is mirrored in the poetic pattern.

As in surf in the sea, the rhythm of many Ginans shows a break in stillness, hence motion, disturbance; yet the break is but a moment followed by restored repose, a restored fusion. And the same sequence is repeated. What we have here is an idea born of, or borne by, something deeper than an idea: something which we can only call 'rhythm'. The rhythm is what gives shape to the idea – turns the idea into thought. Basically, of course, it is the music of the poetry. The melody and the sense are intertwined. In the rise and fall of the melodic patterns, in variations of pitch, in the repetition of lines during recitation, in variations in oral performance, in time and shifts in accent, we catch the rhythm of the thought alongside (and in) the rhythm of the sound. Sometimes in a pattern reminiscent of the surf in the sea, with its simple, climactic rises and rests, its regular cadences, we hear the very pulse-beat of a living, unfolding, religious experience.

It is of course impossible for a verbal translation to convey these qualities. But the quality of living religious experience may be gleaned from the words. As one of many such examples whose syntax gives the sense of a religious experience, so that the poetry is less the *record* of an *experience* than the *recording* of an *experiencing* – an experience in progress – we could refer to the following verses:

> Show your beauteous face, my Lord,
> I am your maid-servant
> Attending on you,
> With joined hands pleading:
> At every breath,
> Be close by me, my Lord.
>
> At every breath,
> Be present in my heart.
> Be not aloof in the space,
> My Lord, of a single breath.
>
> Aloof you are not, my Lord,
> I do not think of you
> As aloof.
> Why, here you are
> Speaking to me
> In the heart
> Of my heart.

The note to this Ginan will analyse it in detail. Here it will suffice to see how the poetry manages to *transcribe* a religious experience in all its *ongoing*, rather than finished, quality.

We might reiterate here the usefulness of attending to linguistic features. In the passage just cited, the I-You mode captures an atmosphere of especial intimacy. Sociologically, this linguistic feature corresponds to face-to-face relationships – relations characteristic of (ideal) families and small communities. When a community, a group of worshippers, recite a hymn in an I-You mode, the dyad becomes a triad. 'We', the reciters, speak with the 'I' of the hymn, in this way becoming joined to that 'I'. When some of the major Pirs, like Sadardin and Hasan Kabirdin, are invoked in the Ginans as saviours or interceders, it is this linguistic feature which grounds this conception.

Still, the 'I', the Pir, the authorial self in the Ginans, remains distinct from the 'I' and 'We' of the follower(s). At times, however, there is a near-mystical effacing of all such distinctions. At such times, a remarkable power is released. When the entire, assembled audience becomes a chorus, when the authorial self in the hymn, and the individual voices in the congregation all merge into a single voice, when the utterance of each becomes one utterance, and the hearts of all beat as one, the resulting voice rises with surpassing power. The words then speak directly from the soul. They are simple words – simple in meaning, simple in their grammar: single nouns, single verbs, without auxiliaries, without complexities of tense or mood. The sentences too are short, direct, simple, free from qualifying clauses. Everything in the world is put into abeyance while prayer, a cry from body and soul – one of the primordial forms of human utterance – takes over. A 'we', which is a perfect fusion of all separate 'I's, calls out, in unison, to a divine 'You'. And what is uttered is a plea harping on the most elemental of human spiritual needs:

> Show me the Good,
> My lord,
> And make me quit the Bad.
> For both
>   are in your hands.
> From you there's always grace,
> Mine
>   are the sin and error.

There is an absoluteness about this utterance: absolute simplicity, absolute concentration, absolute sincerity. The words are straight from the spiritual core of life. They must surely count among that class of religious lyrics, in the collective heritage of mankind, which move us because they speak from and to the soul, bypassing all psychological and intellectual digressions.

Yet the emotion has the sharpest of edges. There's nothing soft, maudlin, or sentimental. The emotion is crystalline, for so are the concepts. 'Show me the Good! Make me quit the Bad!' This is not 'ethics', nor 'morality'. It is the core from which all ethics and morality flow. In comparison to this cry for knowledge of good and evil, all ethical discourse seems feeble and derivative. Only a mind in tune with the essentials, one which is 'naive' in the best sense of the word, unencumbered by emotional or intellectual 'sophistication', can find its way so quickly and so directly to the core of humanity's spiritual neediness. There is no perceived need here to *define* the 'Good' and the 'Bad', no need to *interpret*, no need to qualify, explain, elucidate. There is merely the cry, the call, the prayer, to *show*, to *reveal*. But what a world is present in this 'merely'! How much is already presupposed in this ability to make this plea! For, this cry, this form of speech, rests on the gift of a relationship, a bond between man and his God. If these words speak of a *need*, the need for the 'Good' and the 'Bad' to be shown, they are not the words of a soul enclosed in solitude, but a soul confidently linked in a relationship with the soul of the universe. 'Show me' implies something which is wanting. But the ability to say 'show me' implies the prior presence of a secure relationship. It is the 'givenness' of this bond between the soul and its Maker, which enables a plea for knowledge of good and evil, a knowledge which gives to human life its final meaning, to be uttered in such minimal terms, and in such a direct voice.

And this voice is a collective one, where the burden of individuality is, however momentarily, put aside. The entire congregation becomes a single subject, giving voice, in the moment of collective utterance, to the soul's cry for knowledge and deliverance. This effect is hard to reconstruct from a verbal text, being familiar only to someone who might have witnessed the moment of utterance, when choral volume, lyrical pattern and verbal meaning become one.

It was said above that this literature, like all its analogues, represents a literary and social protest against the stifling of the inner voice, the ossification of the spirit in routinised religion. What we see in this literature is a trace, albeit faint in a purely verbal text – and still more faint in translation into a remote language – of this living moment. It is a voice which in its time came from the inner depths of a people who were inspired by men with the gift of the spirit. That is why it carries, to this day, echoes of a rare, powerful candour and directness of feeling.

Before such directness, the activity of secondary interpretation and commentary, which is no better than a filter, a mediator, is humbled. It feels obliged to lay down its arms, so that, the atmosphere having been cleared of its din, something of the original voice may be heard again.

Miscellaneous
Ginans

(1)

Lord of mine,

Wanting as we are,
Wanting,
And lacking in our rites,
We have our hopes in You.

Lord of mine,

What is green is green,
And green,
Green too
Is what is parched.
If only Your eyes
Were to rest on it,

O Lord of mine.

Lord of mine,

What is sweet is sweet,
And sweet,
Sweet too
Is the bitter stuff.
For the fruits
Of the Master's word
Are all too sweet,

O Lord of mine.

Full are the lakes, full,
Full to the brim.
But not having the word,
How should we drink?

When You poured,
We raised it to our head.
As You bade us do,
So we did,

O Lord of mine.

(2)

The five
    are in hot pursuit of you.
Be sure, merchant,
    to take true provisions with you.
Make lots of gain in the world:
Ahead,
    the Lord will demand a reckoning.

Your sack of bones is filled
    with a fire.
Five bullocks
Are busy filling
    firewood.
Make sure, merchant,
    to take a water-cask with you:
Ahead,
    none will hand water to another.

Of food for the way
    make sure you take enough:
Ahead,
    there's no shop, no *vāṇiyā* in sight.

Gathered at the meal now
    are your family and kin.
But there ahead,
    none will know another.

False, false
    is the woman of your house:
Seeing you off,
    only to return home.

These words
    are of Pir Shams.
Make sure, merchant,
    to take provisions of truth with you.

(3)

In the mulberry-shaped realm
The king sits
Resplendent.
Morning and evening,
Evening and morning,
Each day,
Sing, sing his praises.

Sing, sing the praise of the immaculate one.
Satagur Sohodev shows the road.
Guide of twelve crores, Pir Sadardin
Points the way.

Sing, sing the praise of the immaculate one.

Known all too well to the sage
Is the unuttered
Utterance.
Eighty-four lakh wanderings of the soul
It has laid to rest.

Known all too well to the sage
Is the immortal secret.
To a good seventy-one generations
It has brought
Deliverance.

Sing, sing the praise of the immaculate one.

Numerous are the instruments
Tuned and untuned, all ablast.
See how the world shies away
Seeing in its midst
The inscrutable form.

Sing, sing the praise of the immaculate one.

The rites of *khaṭ darshan*
Are worship
Of the void.
Devoid
Of access
To the secret
Of the true path.

Follow the true path, brothers,
Which has brought good tidings
To the souls
Of infinite millions.

Be mindful, my brothers
Who are well-minded.
Says Gur Sohodev: make,
Make your earnings now.

Says Pir Sadardin: listen,
O faithful ones,
This mindless world knows nothing
Of the king's mystery.

Sing, sing the praise of the immaculate one.

(4)

The Lord is Almighty,
Who made
The entire universe.
O Allah,
On you relies
The universe entire.

This mortal frame,
Half-baked, mound
Of dust:
In the dust
Will the dust
Merge and mingle.

The darkest of dens
Will be its tenement.
Ants will pick
And feed on the flesh.

Says Pir Sadardin:
It's the truthful
Who will reap the fruits.

(5)

Primordially
Was brought forth the Void.
From the Void
Was brought forth the Word.

He will proceed to hell,
He who sports the earring,
But has no hold
Over his self.

He smears ash,
Makes people fall at his feet,
But knows nothing
Of the Word of perfection.

He blows the horn,
And splits the ear,
But knows nothing
Of the divine Word.

He wears his hair long,
A wild and shaggy mat,
But knows nothing
Of salvation's mystery.

The sixty-eight shrines
Are rock and water –
You will gain nothing there.

Says Pir Indra Imamshah,
Listen, my *jogi* friend, if only
You found a master,
Your problems
Would come to an end.

(6)

Speak cool words –
Cool and sweet,
Pleasing
To the congregation.

Go the way of truth
In everything you do.
Then, truly, the Lord
Will be fond of you.

In whose heart the Shah resides,
For him there's no joy eating.
In whose heart the Master resides,
There's no sleep.
Quit sleeping,
O brave one, reflect
On the wisdom divine.

Grandfather,
Whatever happens,
Don't marry me off
To the common folk.

Let me rather stay
A spinster.

If you must marry me off,
                    grandfather,
Give me away to a true sage:
              someone
Who will tide me across.

In an all too narrow street
    I came upon
       my Master.
What was I to do?
I had relations to keep up
With sundry folk.
On the pretext
Of a thorn in my foot,
I bend low, my hand
      saluting
       my Master.

Not every other wood
Yields sandalwood.

Not every other pond
Yields lotus blooms.

So said Pir Sadardin:
The Master's words
Will never,
Never ever turn out wrong,

(7)

What has risen, will set.
What has bloomed, will fade.
Built houses will fall.
He who is born
               will die.

O my heart,
But you are greedy indeed.
Seduced by show
And allure.
It is but a four-day show,
Sure to end in dust.

The jasmine began to wilt,
The drawing-rope snapped.
The bullocks
Came to a stop.   Gone
Was the drawer of water.

Millionaires, crown-princes,
Millions of them,
Are gone.
At one time
Ruling the realm,
Seated in high balconies,
Now smouldering,
To ashes consigned.

Whose is the child,
Whose the offspring?
Whose
Is the mother,
Whose the father?

At the end of it all,
It remains
To go all alone.
Together
With merit and sin.

Said Saiyad Mohamedshah:
Come along, come with me.
Let us go,
Let us redeem our gains,
All recorded, all
In Satagur's hands.

(8)

How is one to know
That one has met
        the true guide?
Look into the heart and see.
See how the neem-tree
Gives off the scent
        of sandalwood.

In that wood lives our beloved,
The wood that gives out the scent
        of sandalwood.
Come, my friends, come
Let's go to that wood,
That there be joy in our hearts.

He who gives his heart
Gives all.
My brave friends,
Be awake all the time.
So said Pir Shams:
Then you'll be among
The thirty-three crores.

(9)

A million felicitations to him –
  he who brings the tidings
  of the Lord's a-coming.
Who, after all,
Had the luck to find
The five maids' beloved Lord?

What untold times have flown,
What ages long,

    searching,
    awaiting,
    looking for the Lord!

A garland drapes the Lord's neck,
  studded
  with rubies and diamonds.
To whom he likes, he gives of them.
For his heart
Is vast as the seas.

My Lord is clever, all-aware.
He is the sovereign,
He, the *diwān* himself.
  Trusting him,
  they have stayed still,
  unwavering –
The earth and the skies.

Till such times
As this world lasts,
I shall remain
His maid-servant –
  at every step
  waiting on his word,
  emulating
The moon and the sun.

So said Pir Sadardin:
If only someone
Could instruct our hearts:
>
>What's the gain
>in washing clothes?
>The heart –
>let the heart be washed!
>That's where there's gain
>>to be had.

What untold times have flown,
What ages long,
>
>>searching,
>>awaiting,
>>looking for the Lord!

Bring forth, bring forth the straw
And stack up the pyre.
                    For gone
Is the swan,
                    left lying
Is the dust.

Foul
        is the body,
Not worth your pride.
There's a little while
To live,
In the end, to die.

Churning and churning
                        the dust,
Palaces were put up,
Good for nothing in the end.

A fort huge as Laṅka,
A moat
        huge as the sea.
And Rāvaṇ, lord of all these:
Yet there was nothing more heard of him.

Sire of a hundred thousand boys,
A hundred and twenty-five thousand girls –
In the house of this Rāvaṇ,
There was not to be found
        a single lamp aglow.

Says Pir Sadardin,
Listen, you
Who are of my very own:
Besides Ali and Nabi
        there's no one else.

(11)

The First, Incomparable Creator-King,
Allah –
   He is the very One
In our hearts.

O Allah!
The heart full of your worship
Is the pure translucent heart.

Recognise the Imam:
      then your faith
Will be the genuine faith,
      yours will be
A place in paradise.

The genuine shine
Is of gold and silver.
Genuine
Are the words of the Master.
The words of the Master
Are words of light.

Satan prayed abundantly,
In the seven skies,
Seven earths,
But waxed proud,
    ignorant,
    unbending before Adam,
    vicegerent of God.

To Yazid's soul
          was allotted
The foul body
            of a dog,
            and so fell
Into wretched misery:
Doomed to roam
The water-girdled tops
Of the Caucasian mounts
In dire torment
Till Judgement Day.

In the depths of hell
There's a flaming well –
Satan's dwelling place.

Where then
Is shelter to be had?
Take note, brothers:
The shelter
Is with Muhammad Mustafā.

So say
Pir Sadardin,
Pir Hasan Kabirdin.
They're my Lord's ministers.

(12)

My Lord fills to the full
            every heart.
Don't you,
            mindless one,
Deem him far.

My Lord to the truthful
                is present
At every breath.
See him as you see
The pupil
            in the eye.

In no way is he far.
Whoever thinks him far,
His deeds are askew,
                one and all.

The three domains
My Lord
            fills to the full.
Consider him
As the blossom's inner scent.

As the scent in the blossom,
So is my Lord.
Don't you,
            mindless one,
Deem him far.

In every heart
My Lord is evident.
Consider him
As the cream in the milk.

My Lord fills to the full
            every heart.
Close at hand,
Closer still.

Sun and moon,
Wind and rain,
                    none
Is peer to my Lord.

My Lord fills to the full
                    every heart.
Don't you,
            mindless one,
Deem him far.

(13)

Of goods and treasures
You have piled an abundance.
Of it, nothing
Is yours.

The pomp, the palaces,
All of it, you'll forgo,
Making the wilderness
                your den.

Why, my heart, why,
O why do you sleep
At this hour
                of remembrance
                of the King,
                of the Lord?
My heart, why,
O why are you asleep?

Time's shadow
Looms over the head
Of saint and sage.
Take heed now
While there's time.
Forgetting now, you'll only fall
Into countless rounds.

This world is all false.
Do not think: it's mine.
Let go of delusion,
Fix your mind on the divine,
Seek, seek
In your inner depths.

Draw in the light
Into your depths.
But for the Master,
It's pitch-black night.
Says Pir Gulmalishah:
Learn, my heart,
        learn,
Make the remembrance now.

O my heart, why,
Why are you asleep?

(14)

Know your
Self,
O devotees, take
The Lord's name.

Checking the five,
Bring the mind
In check.
O devotees,
Turn the heart
To *ilallāh*.

Imbued
With righteousness,
The devotees,
Coming together,
Earning
The earnings pure,
Were as light
                merged
Into light.

Merging,
They were immortal,
Taking
Into their being
The light divine.

Now listen, O devotees –
This love of the world!
In what sorts of affairs
Are your hearts enmeshed!

In greed
And covetousness
The mind is lured away
From the faith's way.

Falling in
With the mind's whims,
O devotees,
Such were the ones scorched
In enticement's flames.

Realise this,
O devotees,
In your inner depths.
Then the heart
Will be pure as the moon.

Follow the Guide
With all your mind.
The Lord is present
In the heart
At every breath.

Says Pir Imamdin,
Listen to these words,
O sages:
In the brow's cave
There shines
The light sublime.

(15)

You are the First,
You are the Last,
    You,
    You alone
Are my Lord.

    You
Are the Apparent,
    You
Are the Hidden.
    You,
Such as You are,
    You alone
Are my Lord in truth.

(16)

Listen, listen, O faithful,
This is what *Kalajug* is like,
This is what it is like,
Kalajug is come at last.

Long days did we wait,
Now at last,
At long last
The last days are come.

After many a day,
Many a day at last,
The time of Ali Shah
Is come at last.

The Lord will exact
A reckoning.
Keep your spirit steady.
Let it steady, steady be.

But for the Pir
There is no paradise:
Know this to be true.
For sure,
Know it to be true.

Say the Word each day,
The creative Word,
Recognise
The creative Word.

There stands
The good ark
of Ali Shah.
There rush the crowds
To Ali Shah's ark.
There goes the rush
Of multitudinous crowds.

Whoever climbs into the ark,
Is ours. For sure,
He's ours.

Seeing Ali Shah,
The heart was steeped in joy.
Let it be known,
Steeped in joy were our hearts.

Pir Shams gives you
The true report.
Know this to be true,
For sure,
Know it to be true.

(17)

Be warned,
            be warned,
Sharpen your mind
         and be warned.
Till you breathe your last,
         be warned.
For where there was the wish,
        but worship
           did not come to be,
The creature rose and left
         despondent.

Whoever missed the essence
Of the Pir's words of wisdom,
Ignorant creature,
He was born
        for nothing.
For nothing
Did the sinner undergo
His rounds of rebirth.

Take this world
To be an emporium
Of stores and stalls.
And in every age
There was trade to be made.
Make your bargains
If you have the flair,
Or else you will only make
The empty rounds.

Tired was the day,
Tired too the night.
The gorgeous body,
                    tiring,
Succumbed at last.
Mother earth entire
Tired in the end.
But vile illusion was one
Who stayed on, untiring,
To the end.

Taking the Lord to be true,
Worship Him
With trust in your heart.
Says Pir Sadardin,
There's no way you will lose
If you play your cards with care.

(18)

From a land afar
The merchant has come along.
Get together and make deals with him.

Bearing pearls,
The merchant has come over.
Go, pick up the precious pearls.

Do not trade with the one
Who gives up jewels
For the sake of glass.

Sitting, sleeping, going about,
Take the Lord's name,
Take the Lord's name.

Make a fair profit
Which the fire will not scorch,
        the wind will not sway,
        the waters will not sink,
        the king will not tax.

Give away in the Lord's name
What is dearest in your home.
Giving a grain here,
You will take a hundred
And twenty-five thousand-fold
        over there.

As for the blind,
He will not see the moonlight.
Being told of it,
He won't believe.

Throwing open the treasury,
There sits my Lord.
Listen to him speak
Of what is high
And what is low.

With scales in hand,
My Lord is ready:
Bring out your goods,
Let's tell their worth.

Pir Hasanshah said these words:
Believe truly in our Lord.

A Scent of Sandalwood

(19)

What are we to say to him
Who reads and knows?
Without deeds
What fruits are to be had?

The road to deliverance
Is a hard one.
How are we to get
To the city
Of immortals?

Serving the Lord
And Master
Is the way to the city
Of immortals.

Let there be a seat in the eye
For the Master.
Let there be a love immense
For the Lord.
Let a diamond be set
In the centre of the necklace
Of rubies and pearls.
Let not go of such a lot
For the sake of a little.

Let not go
            of love for the Lord.

Pain and pleasure
In the body
Are sure to come,
Sure to go.
But the true faith –

Let not go of it
From the heart.

108

Says Pir Sadardin:
Listen, O brave brethren,
Be sure to fulfil the vows
Tendered in the womb.

(20)

Said the proprietor to the agent:
Listen now, go. Go and make
Handsome deals.
What more can I say to you:
Be smart, be wise,
Let us see you back
Having made
Ample gains.

Earn your way at the Pir's behest,
Taking to heart
Nabi Muhammad's precepts fair.
Go, go wisely. Let's see you back
Having made
Handsome gains.

Many a day you spent
In that dark, darkest realm.
Every now and then you were saved
From hazards small and great.
Unknowing, you were fed
With needed fare.
Parentless, you were looked after.

For nine months long
Borne in the womb,
At long last, you were unbound
By Nabi Muhammad's grace.

Giving your word you went forth
Into the world.
Seeing its alluring ways
You lost your head.

What a thriving store you set up there!
How you appointed yourself
To the proprietor's very place!

False was your balance,
All too false,
With that hook in the rod.
Falsely weighted
Were your scales.

And how you gorged yourself!
Milk and meal,
Butter, sugar and nectar!
And on top of it all,
Swills of refreshing drink.

How you spread
On those couches,
Cushions and sheets
Of the finest weave!
How, lying on them,
You had yourself fanned
With the softest breeze!

Then came summons
From the proprietor.
Let's go, agent,
Let's go
With the utmost speed.

In what haste you left!
Lock and key
Left in the store,
Empty-handed
You made your way.

Kith and kin,
Arrived and assembled.
Bidding the creature farewell,
They turned their backs,
Sending him on the way
With his vice and virtue's share.

Says the proprietor to the angel:
Listen now, go. Go and fetch
This creature's books.

There they sit,
Proprietor and agent,
Tallying the books.
How the wretched soul
Shivers
In terror's grip.

Page after page,
The creature's sins
Are etched in bold.
Of virtue, there's not to be seen
The tiniest trace.

Says Pir Sadardin:
Lord, we fed ourselves off you –
Only with your mercy now
Can the soul go free.

(21)

Full to the brim,
Full and overflowing
Are the lakes of truth,
                    full
Of the fine, immortal draught.

Set up the banks,
O brave brothers,
Set up the banks of love.
Set up the banks to the lakes
                    of truth.

When the prince of swans
            took to the swim,
            how promptly did the storks flee –
Here, there, and everywhere.

Says Pir Sadardin, listen O faithful ones,
            you too shall swim
With the twelve crores.

(22)

Plunging into the three-streamed realm,
The cowering self quakes.
Embark with a vow of faith,
Keep your spirit firm,
Steady all the way.

Look out, think well ere you speak,
Keep faith with the Lord,
And walk the way of truth.
Keep stocking up virtue:
Why stock up worldly wares?
That way
How should you hope
To cross ashore?

Why do you keep giving up,
Turning coward,
Proving unable
To bear the load?
     The sovereign Lord,
     this time in his tenth guise,
     is due
     to demand reckoning.

Look, look out,
Think well ere you speak.
Walk, walk the way of truth.
Keep faith with the sovereign King.

This coin that you made,
Of an amalgam of lead
And coppery melt,
Floated on the bazaar,
Will not make it far.
     For no hand will deign to bear
     the coin it knows is fake.

The genuine coin
Is struck in the mint.
That's the real coin.
    Floated on the bazaar,
    none will declare it fake.

Look, look out,
Think well ere you speak.
Walk, walk the way of truth.
Keep faith with the sovereign King.

The Lord has come to tell
The true from the fake,
As the scriptures testify.
All too thoroughly
Will he examine,
Weighing, melting,
Probing to the core.

Those who come out fake
Will surely make their way
To hell's dammed assembly.
To the true
He will hand the treasury,
Paradise,
The vision divine.

The debris of three ages past
Has come along its way to the fourth.
In egoistic excess
The world will decay,
As the woman of the house
Makes her way
To an alien man's embrace.

So said Pir Sadardin,
Be watchful, O devotees,
Be true
In devotion to the Lord.
Then He will grant you
Paradise,
And the vision divine.

(23)

In my heart he lives, Allah
The Creator, He who fashioned
Nature's eternal scheme.

Say, O m*ullāh*! Say,
O *qāzi*! Who was it
Who made this universe?

From this dust
Was this entire world made.
Who shall we say
In all this
Is the Hindu? And the Musalman?

The Hindu is he who proceeds
To the sixty-eight shrines.
The Musalman, he who proceeds
To the mosque.

Not Hindu, nor Musalman
Knows my Lord.
My Lord is seated
Pure, immaculate.

My mind
Is my prayer-mat.
Allah, my *qāzi*.
My body, a mosque.

Seated within,
I say my *namāz*.
What can the fool know
Of my prayer?

If food comes my way,
It is grace. If not,
It's a fast.
That is the way
I think on my Lord.

He who knows these mysteries,
Is the faithful one,
Walking straight
On wisdom's way.

It all became clear
Through knowledge
And contemplation.
Search, search –
And you will surely find.

Said Pir Shams, listen,
O faithful ones:
Without a Pir,
How should you hope
To cross ashore?

(24)

Warriors
Who used to break up mountains with their hands,
And drink up the oceans,
Have rolled in dust.
Who then are you
That are proud?

Take the name of God,
O heedless one!
Transient is this world.
Take the name of God,
O greedy one!
Transient is this world.

Here today, gone tomorrow,
O creature!
Gone in the twinkling of an eye.
Gone
With the morsel
Still in mouth.

Take the name of God,
O heedless, greedy creature,
Transient is this world.

Not a moment
Did he tarry, the one
With whom you were just
Laughing, chatting.
Tied now in a bundle,
Carried away
On the shoulders,
Topsy-turvy.

Take the name of God,
O heedless one!
Transient is this world.
Take the name of God,
O greedy one!
Transient is this world.

(25)

At the hour of light
            imbibe
The light.
            Let delight
Fill your mind.

At the hour of bloom,
                of light,
Make your bonds
With the Shah and Pir.

Wake, wake, brothers,
There gives birth
                the night.
Be alert, O brothers,
There delivers
                the night.

Wash, dress, be worthy
And adore
The unscriptable Lord.
Cast away
Ill-gotten gains
And adore the Lord
At the hour
            of light.

Adore the worthiest
Of guests,
The unscriptable Lord.
For all else
Are ghost-haunted
Habitations.

In the remaining
Hours of the night,
Wake, wake, brothers.
Waking at the hour
            of light,
Adore
The unscriptable Lord.

Says Pir Sadardin, this age
Is the last
         of the night.
How few are the heroes
Who know the path
Of truth!

Wake, wake, brothers,
There gives birth
         the night.
Be alert, O brothers,
There delivers
         the night.

(26)

Family, relations, husband,
All I abandoned.
Tied my heart to my Lord,
Joined my mind to You.

Says the prophet to the Lord,
Don't, don't go far by a jot.
When the agony is come,
Be within my sight, my Lord.

Stretched on a mat,
Spread on a bed
Of thorns, I have not
A moment's sleep
While on every leaf above
The beloved
Teases my soul.

Says the prophet to the Lord,
Don't, don't go far by a jot.
When the agony is come,
Be within my sight, my Lord.

(27)

Study, at every breath,
Study, and see for yourself.

Adore the Lord with every breath.
My Lord is well by your side.
He is close by you,
Nothing short,
Have full trust in him.

He resides in every pore:
The Spiritual,
Indestructible Lord.

At every breath
Stay in the wisdom divine:
Study, study
And see for yourself.

That heart which is full
Of the unuttered utterance
Is the heart full of light.

Says Imam-Begum:
Whoever acts thus
Will live in paradise.

(28)

Dying is for sure,
Be wary in the world.

Well-appointed is the body's fort,
The five senses are its worth.

Five thieves are at large in the body's land:
Be wary, to your mind's root, as you tread.

A mighty dread haunts your body's edifice:
One day Time
Will shatter it to bits.

Give alms, charity, at every breath,
Patience is the root of faith.

So says Imam-Begum,
Listen, brethren,
Close to the Satagur you will stay.

(29)

The Shah's writ has arrived
In *Janpudip*.
The brave Chandan
Has brought it over.

The Shah's writ is read
By Pir Indra Imamdin.
Today my heart
Can barely hold my joy.

Would that I had wings
To fly to the Shah!
Alas, my body will not
Yield to my will.

Would there were bearers
To bear me aloft!
In suchlike musings
I look around
And bide my while.

Pick up the flowers
Strewn by virtuous maids,
Untouched
By *Kalajug's* winds.

The wayfarers
And courtiers,
Loyal to the Shah's word,
Are set out for the court.

The sea roars
Fearfully.
Many a coward there
Gives up his breath.

Tiger and lion
Well-aware of the Shah,
Send the wayfarers
On their way.

The high-peaked mountains
Seem all too fearsome.
Up there blow the ice-cold,
Himalayan winds.

Courtier and wayfarer,
All as one,
Arrive at the court,
In the city of Kahek:
The splendid Kahek,
Where the king of three worlds is enthroned.

Pir Indra Imamdin
Voiced this prayer:
Lord, forgive
The congregation's sins.

(30)

The towering walls,
The flowing stream beneath.
I'm a fish in the stream.
    Come, Lord, come,
    come to the rescue.

For lack of your sight,
I'm all distraught.
Beloved, come home,
    Lord, come
To this devotee
Who neglected his devotions.
Lord, show yourself,
        show
Your beauteous face.

A roomful of sandalwood.
Splendidly carved
        are the doors,
        locked
        with locks of love.
    Come, Lord, come,
    come and undo the locks.

Cast into the cage
        of family,
        relations –
Few are those who know
The anguish in my being.
    Come, Lord, come,
    come to quench
    this raging fever.

Do not harbour
This much wrath, my Lord.
Lord, do show yourself.
Pir Hasanshah beseeches you:
    Come, Lord, come,
    come to the rescue.

(31)

Sire, I am gripped
            by fear,
                fear
    of but one day,
                fear
    of a minute,
                fear
    of a split second.

Shaped of unbaked clay,
The pot gave no sound
As it smashed.

This body is a flower-garden.
Grazing off it
Is a deer.

One day the Lord
Will summon all,
Will take a reckoning
Of every grain.

Says Imam-Begum:
If you take heed
You will be rid
Of fear
Of the time to come.

(32)

My lord,
My heart is fond of you.
I think of no-one else.
None else pleases my heart.
My lord,
My heart is fond of you.

So readily, my lord,
You give me
Whatever I ask of you.
You indulge me
In so many ways,
My lord.

In all four ages,
I went about,
Looking hard.
I found none
To match you, my lord.

My lord, my heart
Is fond of you.

Come, come,
My maiden friends,
Let us go
To view the groom.
He's the one, the beloved
I've attained.

He comes to my home,
The beloved,
He but for whom
A minute is hard to pass.

How should we call him
Unhappy –
He whose lord
Is one such as this?

How should we find fault
With the merciful?
What's written
In our karma
Is what we shall have.

Ram and Raheman
Are but one Deity.
Of this mystery,
The fool is quite unaware.

So said Saiyad Mohamadshah:
I am bonded to you,
My lord.
Leaving you,
At what other door
Am I to knock?

My lord,
My heart is fond of you.
I think of no-one else.
None else pleases my heart.
My lord,
My heart is fond of you.

(33)

Speak sweet words, friends,
Go about humbly,
Patiently.
Never give up love
Of the true faith.

Bring out the bile,
That rancour
In your depths.
Then the Lord will be pleased,
Plenteously.

Be not proud, my friend,
Of this fragile body.
Any day now
It will droop,
Drop to earth.

Dust will mix, mingle
With dust.
Your body will take on
A vermilion tint,
My friend.

The soul is heavenly,
Earthly is the body,
In love
Like the two-day lotus bloom.

The faithful is he, my friend,
Who checks himself.
For what is it to you
To check others, my friend?

The faithful is he, my friend,
Who mends
Where there's a tear.
Heaven-bound
Will be his soul.

He who uncovers
A brother in faith,
Hell-bound
Will be his soul.

By the grace of the Lord
Pir Shams said these words.
What, after all,
Do they have in common –
The body and soul?

(34)

The wasp flits about
The blossom by day,
Is caught
As it folds by night.
Just so, O creature,
This world will pass
While you languish
In untruth.

Remember the Lord in time,
And you will reap the fruits
                              ahead.
In no time will this world
                    pass away.

For the stomach's sake
The creature left the Lord.
Like the fish
Caught
In the net.

The deer in the forest
Hurries along
To where he sees the water –
Seeing the water,
                    not seeing
The poised arrow.

Knowing this well,
The soul fell
For the display.
Seeing the display,
                    not seeing
The pretence.

(35)

Awake, awake,
        be awake,
The Satagur has arrived,
The sixty-eight shrines
are here,
at home's threshold.
The Ganga and Jamna
            are here,
          full and flowing.
Now he who bathes is purified,
While the wicked
Will stay aloof from the Lord.

Diving in the congregation-pond
Pearls invaluable came in hand.
Guard, guard the jewels:
They'll grow manifold in worth.
Learning the truth,
Keep it in the heart,
Telling no-one else.

Slay the ego.
The Master says:
Then you'll be mine;
I'll stitch you on
To my being.
A diamond has come in your hands:
Observe, be wise.

For he who makes deals
Is a businessman,
While he who takes
And will not give,
Is a bankrupt man.

(36)

Show your beauteous face, my Lord,
I am your maid-servant
Attending on you,
With joined hands pleading:
At every breath
Be close by me, my Lord.

At every breath
Be present in my heart.
Be not aloof in the space,
My Lord, of a single breath.

Aloof you are not, my Lord,
I do not think of you
As aloof.
Why, here you are
Speaking to me
In the heart
Of my heart.

My Lord, only you
Know the bounds of your bounds.
You are my great protector, my Lord.

Age after age, my Lord
Redeemed his devotees
(Excellent for ever
Is the path of truth):

Dhruv, Pahelāj, Rukhmugat the king.
Harischandra,Tārārāni, Rohidās the prince:
True to their vow, they were sold
From hand to hand;
The five Pāndavas and Mātā Kuntā,
We should say,
And Sati Dropadi with them too;
The great Pir Sadardin,
Master of twelve crores,
With the infinite crores
Going with Pir Hasan Kabirdin,
To whom the Immaculate Lord gave his hand.

When the Immaculate Lord
Comes to be the groom,
He will be the consort
Of the universal bride.

On that day, my Lord,
Summon me by your side.
Be sure, my Lord,
To take my hand in yours.

Says Imam-Begum: listen, my Lord,
This much, just this much,
Do I ask of you, my Lord.

(37)

Everlasting God,
True and Everlasting.
Present in nine continents
And three worlds,
Sovereign Lord for ever.

He lives in my heart's depths,
My Lord.
Why look for him
Out and around?

Without earnings
There's no salvation:
Ahead, your righteousness
Will be weighed in the balance.

There, Gur Sohodev will rise and tide over,
Will make his followers
Tide over.
They shall tide over,
Those who were true,
Who fulfilled the tithe.

(38)

O brave ones,

Creatures are carved of clay.
Turn your mind to He who made
You and me,
The King of souls.

Be concerned:
Alerting yourself,
Avert lust and rage,
Be concerned with your soul.

The first to forget
Were the common herd of men.
The common herd
Are the ignorant lot,
Heedless of their souls.

O brave ones, hurry on,
Hurry on to where you came,
For to that very home
You and I,
I and you
Are due.

So said Pir Satagur Sohodev,
O brave ones, on your lot
The Eternal God has smiled.
Go, go there and mingle
In the festival
Of thirty-three crores.

(39)

Hearken to this word of mine:
I have come
Onto a proper path.

Whose daughter are you?
In which man's house
Are you now a spouse?

Truth's daughter is who I am,
Child to contentment.
A spouse
In an earthly man's house.

The earthly man
I left asleep.
The children
I left rocking.
The milk
I left boiling.
Leaving all, shunning
All other doors,
I have come
To the door divine.

For the sake of the soul
I left all, surrendering
To You.

Truth's garment
And contentment's cord,
Through consciousness
I tied in a knot.

Truth's cauldron,
Contentment's pitcher,
And I: the faith's
Water-drawing rope.

Says Pir Shams:
I come contracted
To a pledge of old.

(40)

Now I am in love with you,
                    my Lord,
My heart is stricken now
            with love for you.
Let eye look into eye,
Now that I am in love, now,
                    with you, my Lord.

Lift the veil, let us come
Face to face.
Show your gently smiling face,
                    my Lord,
Now, now that I am in love with you,
                    my Lord.

For your face I am all athirst,
                    my Lord,
Grant me the gift,
That gift of your sight,
Now that I am in love,
That I am in love with you,
                    my Lord.

Don't sulk on me, beloved,
Keep company with me,
Now that I am in love with you,
                    my Lord.

This, your lover, will go
Wherever you go.
Let there be friendship in your heart,
Now that I am,
That I am in love with you,
                    my Lord.

Listen, O handsome one,
Oh, you reticent one!
Let there be mercy in your heart,
Now that I am in love with you,
                    my Lord.

For your secret I am mad,
My Lord.
Let it be!
Let reason
Be overcome by love!
Now
That I am in love with you,
                    my Lord.

When the face was seen
There was joy at heart.
Pir Shams told the tale:
Now I am in love with you,
                    my Lord,
My heart is stricken now
            with love for you.

(41)

The banks have burst.
The waters overflowed.
There's none about
To mend the dams.
None around
To rein in
The panicked cow.
No cowherd
In the community –

O good brothers,
A great discord
Has erupted in *Kalajug*.
Yes, brothers,
A great discord is rife
In *Kalajug*.

Words of learning, wisdom,
Scripture,
Have no readers any more.
Books and scrolls
Are stacked away,
Their content lost
From memory.

Mothers have renounced
Pity for the child.
The hearts of men have grown
Selfish.
Bonds of love, affection
Will loosen fast;
Bonds between brothers,
Dissolve.

O good brothers,
A great discord is rife
In *Kalajug*.

There's none will treat
               the teacher
As honoured guest.
The subjects will not heed
The king's decree.
The fair maid
Will forswear her shame.
The four mines
Will in horror quake.

The king
Will prove tyrant incarnate,
Wreaking
Iniquities without end.
Day will transgress day.
Famine
Will rage at last.

The guardian
Will prove a thief.
The people, all at a loss.
The rivers, nine hundred
And ninety-nine of them,
Will dry away. The bull
Will shrug
The earth off its back.

O good brothers,
A great discord
Has erupted in *Kalajug.*
Yes, brothers,
A great discord is rife
In *Kalajug.*

The demons
Have set up a dispute –
Beware, O brothers,
The roads to virtue
Are blocked.
Blighted is the faith.

Inhabited cities
Will be laid to waste.
Anarchy will reign.
The mystical arts
Will fall into neglect.
The essence and flavour
Of it all drained low
To the bowels of the earth.

None will rise
To virtuous rites.
All will rise
To satisfy
The stomach's selfish need,
Maligning
Their ancestral ilk.

None will minister
To the orphan's need,
Nor the mendicant's.
At but one invitation
To weddings and festivities,
All and sundry will rush,
Uninvited, to the feast.

In the midst of celebration
They will start a fight
And head for the court of law.
All at loggerheads,
None will call at another's home.

They will violate
          mother,
               father,
                    teacher.
Improper designs of the heart
Will lurk under every roof.

Son will outdare father.
The pupil
Will override the teacher.

The clerk will outdo the boss.
Women will boss over men.
The crook
Will out-smart the saint
And take him to court.

O good brothers,
A great discord
Has erupted in *Kalajug.*
Yes, brothers,
A great discord is rife
In *Kalajug.*

Plants of all species
Will wither,
Root and branch.
Trees bearing wholesome fruit
Will shrivel.
What'll remain
Will be unfit to eat.

Among women there'll be none
                          faithful.
Among men there will be none
                          pure-eyed.
None will reveal himself.
None will trust another.

None will visit
Houses of worship.
None will exhibit
Miraculous feats.
There'll be none
To plead the cause
Of the suffering.

Those who have knowledge
Will act proud.
Night and day
The entire world
Will lie asleep.

Said Pir Sadardin,
Be warned:
Three entire ages have gone by,
Now has come
Kalajug's time.

Yes, brothers,
A great discord is rife
In *Kalajug*.
O good brothers,
A great discord
Has erupted in *Kalajug*.

(42)

O saviour of my soul,
Do not go far.
    Come, come and take your place
    In this comely shape,
    A home fit for you.

When in a brief, matchless respite
I repair to bed,
    In love I draw close
    To my beloved:
    My woes, out of mind.

On the swing,
Breathing in, breathing out,
There's a surge in my being,
My beloved by my side.

To whom is one to tell
The tale of longing
For the beloved one?
Till a sage comes along,
It's for the best
To keep it to oneself.

The Maker of worlds was the one
Who came to save.
Seizing his skirt,
Pir Sadardin crossed
The colossal seas.

(43)

Adore the Satagur,
Waking
At night's midpoint,
Meeting up in congregation.

For in the congregation
The Lord and Master reside
In manifest shape,
The *nakalanki's* very guise.

For this reason wake,
                    wake,
If for two seconds;
While on the head loom
The shadows
Of death's demon.

For surely you will die,
Bound as you are
In illusion's fetters.
Why, but why
Do you spin around
On fruitless rounds?

The times now are dire.
Listen, my ascetic souls,
This hymn, rich in meaning,
Is told by Pir Sadardin:
Be warned,
Be warned
While there is time.

A Scent of Sandalwood

(44)

The scarlet lion forgot himself –
Amid sheep, a sheep
He came to be.

Lost in such delusion,
You forgot your life.
Oh, quit the delusion,
And take Ali's name.

Ali it is,
And Ali forever it will be.
Bear in the heart
Words as these.

Shake off the delusion,
So that the lion
Is restored,
Purged of sheep-love.

Plunged in ignorance
Was the soul,
In self-obsession
Losing the loved one,
Waxing proud of a sudden.

Oh, quit the delusion,
And take to Ali's name.

Take to the company
Of the perfect guide.
Gone then will be ignorance,
And you'll grow alert
To the heart's murmur.

Oh, do quit the delusion,
And take Ali's name.

Conquering delusion,
You'll come to know God.
Will come to know
The 'you' of yourself.

Says Pir Shams,
Abide by these words.
Oh, quit the delusion,
And take,
Take to Ali's name.

For Ali it is,
And Ali forever it will be.

From the *Saloko Nāno*
(Pir Sadardin)

From the Saloko Nāno *(Pir Sadardin)*

The entire world says
Beloved, beloved!
But the beloved
Is had by none.
If the beloved
Were to be had
By lip-service,

There would be no dealing in heads.

Bugs and beasts too cry
For the beloved
And none attain
The beloved.
If the beloved
Were to be had
Through lip service,

The stork would be as the swan.

Storks and swans
Are distinct, yet like-seeming.
The stork feeds at whim,
While the swan
On a diet of pearls.

Glass beads and gems
Are distinct
And when appraised
Reveal their worth.
Purchased glass
Fills the poison-store,
While the gem
Yields sparkling light.

The master-less one
And the master-guided
Are distinct, yet like-seeming.
The master-less soul
Feeds on junk,
While the master-guided,
On the name of the Lord.

The name was said countless times.
Absent
Were pangs of love.
It was all
       plaster laid on dust,
       the mere beat
       of punctured drums.

From the Saloko Nāno *(Pir Sadardin)*

How will they cross ashore –
The master,
    with a sack on his head,
The pupil,
    with a load on his head,
Both of them
    seated in a metal boat?

Where the master is blind
And the pupil
Good for nothing,
Self-opinionated,
Stubborn at heart –
No, there's not for them

Salvation after death.

The world is a vast raging sea.
On the head
    sits a heavy load.
If you seat yourself
    in the boat of love,
Satagur
    will sail you across.

Make a boat
    of God's name,
    filling it
    with the weight of truth.
If now the wind of love were to rise,
Satagur will sail it across.

We came to this world
Carrying salvation's secret clue.
Pomp, pleasure, office –
They had it all.
But few –

Oh, all too few,
Proved a lover's worth.

Their luck ran out,
They who observed
                austerities,
                pilgrimages,
                countless alms.
Having relished paradise,
Down they plunged –

They who never knew
The light divine.

Brahmins, Yogis, Shaivites –
                all wander astray.
How can that soul get to be
                immortal,
Who never got to know the true guide?

From the Saloko Nāno *(Pir Sadardin)*

From the four mines you came forth,
And sank
     into a huge forgetfulness.
Thanks to merit
Earned in previous births,
You attained human form.

You bore human form,
Yet none knows
Salvation's clue.
How dare the ruby boast
So long as it stays
Unpierced at the core?

Time's falcon
Hovers on your head.
Don't you count
On whatever. Only,
Keep the beloved in your heart,
In the manner
Of the high risen sun.

Untimely
You came into the world
Stumbling
Through the four mines.
Hatched from a half-formed egg,
You never saw
The risen sun.

The sun rose,
And all was light.
Gone was the night.
Even so,
Through the nine constellations
Shines the Lord,
Like the morning's
Risen sun.

When the sun is overhead
All call it day,
None says night.
Even so,
Satagur is the saviour of the age.
There's no salvation
Through another.

Light
        made the world.
And light
        built the skies.
From the light
There sprang a light:
Satagur was its name.

Where in the heart
The light of faith
                is ablaze,
Ignorance
        keeps at bay.
What can they do,
Powers of the dark,
Where there shines
Satagur's light?

From the Saloko Nāno *(Pir Sadardin)*

Seek out
The manifest form,
And trust him with a truthful heart.
For when iron kisses
The philosopher's stone,
In an instant
It turns to gold.

Gold and silver
Are the true stuff,
Subjected
To the fiery test.
But with a base alloy added,
How will the mixture ever melt?

The wasp and the larvae
Are distinct,
Abiding in the nest.
Suffering the wasp's sting,
The larvae
Comes to be as the wasp.

Everyone dies a false death
And none dies the true way.
He who dies
In wisdom divine
Has no more deaths to die.

You came over,
Oblivious soul,
In the vast oblivion
Of ignorance; came
Eighty-four times,
Yet never slew
The furies five.

He who checks the five furies,
Dies to the world.
Making the Satagur
His companion,
He is destined
To the immortal home.

From the Saloko Nāno *(Pir Sadardin)*

The Ganges came its way
From heaven's domain,
Off Vishnu's feet.
Legion streams
Running into it,
Become the Ganges as it is.

The Ganges is a site
For prolific shrines.
But the shrine of shrines,
The Satagur Pir
From the Ganges stays all aloof,
Declaring its waters

Null and void.

Why worship the void?
Honour instead
          the living light.
Till love does not attach
          to the beloved,
The soul will languish
          in the four mines.

Ghost-worship
Is the whole world's way
And dooms its creatures
To colossal rounds.
Having made the jungle
Your residence,
Who will you find there
To show you the way?

Having wandered off
To the jungle,
You were a lost soul.
Who there would show you the way?
If only
In that boundless wild
You were to meet a living soul
You might glimpse
Destination's whereabouts.

Where the world is void,
And blind are the times,
When the void
Worships the void:
Like the orgasm
Of the impotent
Is the immortality
Of such a soul.

From the Saloko Nāno *(Pir Sadardin)*

Barren lands
        get resettled.
And the impoverished
        get rich again.
But consider this marvel
        of marvels:
The dead
        do not get
        to live again.

I looked up the sixty-eight shrines,
And found some of it to be rock
And some of it, water.
What welcome will he find –
A guest in an empty home?

The shrine is face to face
                in the heart.
And in the heart
Is the gate to faith.
Worship the Lord
                in the heart.
                In the heart
Lies deliverance
And the vision divine.

From the Saloko Nāno *(Pir Sadardin)*

Love-worship abides
In the heart,
All attention
Focussed at the core.
Reciting the word
Is its way,
        inhaling,
        exhaling,
     with the ears
     shut to sound.

Take the Lord's name
With every breath
With no thought
Of aught else.
Keep not the beloved
A hair's breadth away;
Be as the wave
Merging into the ocean's depths.

Rise to the *zikr,*
And grasp the gift of night.
When from the navel
The breath takes its start,
Start a talk then
With the beloved Lord.

Kill all expectations
And don the adornment
              of truth.
Paint the eyes with the kohl
              of love,
Make of the beloved
A garland round the neck.

From the Saloko Nāno *(Pir Sadardin)*

As the morning breaks
And the sun rises,
Irradiating
The nine constellations,
Shedding as much light
In every nook
As is needed –

So the beloved resides
In every heart.

The beloved is had
With total love;
Loveless,
He stays far away –
Like the lotus
In the water's midst:
Impervious, its skin.

The entire world says,
Beloved, beloved.
But the beloved
Is had by none.
The lips relate but one story,
While of the beloved's mystery,
None knows a thing.

If the beloved were to be had
By lip-service,
While the head labours
Under a heavy load,
And the heart wanders
Separate from the lips –
Why, a broken boat
Will not make it
To the shore.

They call themselves
Learned pundits of the world,
And make all and sundry
Drink of their feet.
Of salvation's mystery
They know but nothing,
And so they only
Multiply their sins.

They learned a lot
And never took to the right road.
If you run around a lot
You will only fall
Into colossal rounds.

From the Saloko Nāno *(Pir Sadardin)*

On the housetop
Shines the light,
While dark night
Reigns within.
Futile
Are the outward ablutions
When the interior grime
Stays with you all the while.

Taking elixir
Purges poison.
Taking water
Quenches thirst.
Taking a meal
Relieves hunger.
          So,
Taking God's name
Removes pollution.

From the Saloko Nāno *(Pir Sadardin)*

Truth and falsehood
Are distinct –
Tell the difference, you
Who can tell differences.
When that pearl cracked
Being strung,
It lost untold worth.

The world gives ear
To the liar
          and kicks
At the honest man.
When a liar meets up
With a liar,
          together
They will declare
          two and two
          to be five.

Everyone speaks
The collective speech.
And none utters
Words of truth.
They carp and slander all along,
Oblivious of their state
          and so,
Pile karma on their heads.

Karma can all be undone.
Not so, slander
And false imputation.
Nor is adultery undone,
Nor suicide,
Nor too
Infanticide.

He who bears the mark
Of these five forms
Of murder,
Each and every one of them a sin,
Will never ever be immortal
Through he were, day after day,
To sit in the congregation.

They all do penance
And pilgrimage,
And proffer alms
Huge as the earth.
And yet,
Though they bathe in the Ganges,
Never ever
Will their karma be undone.

The five acts of murder
Were denounced in the other world,
And etched
On an iron plate.
Never ever will it fade,
Even as it breaks.
There's no way out then,
But to live out
The allocated fate.

From the Saloko Nāno *(Pir Sadardin)*

So what,
If you made yourself a *satī?*
If you did not smoulder
For the beloved's sake?
Go, go away,
Wretched woman –
Not for love
Did you die.

It is they who died,
Whose unruly selves
         died;
Who made themselves
Low as the earth.
See the wonder of it:
These puppets
Of five organs,
Uttering
The unuttered chant.

Wherever we looked
Through the ages,
We saw the poor.
And of the rich,
We saw but none.
Reckon him as rich,
Who to the beloved
Is bound in love.

Love does not
　　　grow in fields;
Nor is love
　　　sold in shops;
Love arises
　　　in the heart,
　　　and the heart
　　it corrodes,
　　　through and through.

From the Saloko Nāno *(Pir Sadardin)*

They are the worthy ones
Who were as dead,
Their hearts
Ridden with darts.
As for those who are spear-proof,
They're but mountain rocks.

Preaching to the mountain rocks
I made them melt.
But the lost souls,
Bereft of a guide,
Sunk in vast ignorance,
Just wouldn't melt.
Like splinters on the anvil:
In the absence of the guide,
Ineffectual darts.

Where the shafts of passion strike,
Where love inflicts throbbing wounds,
Sleep deserts the eyes,
                              powerless.
For the soul is all-awake,
Losing the entire night,
Calling for the beloved
Till night passes into day.

Being brave,
They gave their heads,
As under an enemy's blows.
Holding their lives cheap,
It is in death
That they'll have their due.

Dancing on the gallows,
The player makes his play,
Treading on a sword-edge,
Lashed and whipped the while.

From the Saloko Nāno *(Pir Sadardin)*

Dear as pearls,
The Lord is obtained
By giving gold.
How is such a Lord
To be abandoned

At the carping of common folk?

Adore the one who is
                ascendant.
Authority is his
Whose turn it is.
What use singing praises
Of the meal
        relished yesterday?

Why relate tales of old?
                Rather probe
The prevailing mystery –
The high-risen, glorious form,
                        shedding
Moonlight into hearts.
Of this glory,
None knows the formula.

The formula of truth
Is best of all.
Proceed in truth.
Those who go about
Lacking in truth,
Will whirl about
On incessant rounds.

In *Kalajug* unsteady is the world.
Those who follow
Words of scripture
Will in a trice
Swim ashore –

As did the five crores
In *Kartājug,*
Total in their faith,
Never letting a defect
Linger in their hearts,
And were straight delivered
By Pahelāj the King;

As did the seven crores,
True followers of truth,
Speaking ill of none,
Delivered
In *Tretājug*
By Harischaṅdra the King;

As did the nine crores
Delivered
In *Duāpurjug*
By the Pāṅdavas
Who froze their flesh
But never let go
Of their truth, constant
In their love of God;

As did the twelve crores,
In *Kalajug,*
Who stayed true,
With Pir Sadardin the true,
              unhesitating
In their devotion
           to the Lord.

From the Saloko Nāno *(Pir Sadardin)*

Pir Sadardin is the true one:
Appreciate this,
O faithful ones,
For in all four ages
All too many souls
Went astray.

– So did Gur Sohodev say.

'A Plea'
(Pir Hasan Kabirdin)

'A Plea' (Pir Hasan Kabirdin)

All hopes
        are on you,
        Enduring lord.
Give a thought to us,
            O our king.
The entire congregation
Is on its feet;
Lord,
Grant your devotees
The kingdom, the home.

These days
        in the tenth guise,
you
    are the saviour-lord.
O my lord,
Bring to mind
The promise of old.
To the universal maid
Grant a groom,
                Enduring lord,
Deliver,
Deliver
        the devotees' souls.

Lord of three worlds,
I find you
        in my heart.
Make knowledge and wisdom
Speak to me.

O my lord,
Emblazon
            on the golden base
Pearls and rubies,
The sumptuous jewels, rubicund.

To you
>   let me be bound in devotion,
>   Enduring lord,
So that wisdom may come to me.
Let my lips form such words
As you deem fit, O my lord.

Show me the Good,
My lord,
And make me quit the Bad.
For both
>   are in your hands.
From you there's always grace,
Mine
>   are the sin and error.

In all earnestness
I ask of you:
Hear out my supplication
And give it attention,
O my lord.
Make me do such deeds
As you please:
Do not then place the blame
On my head.

Have mercy,
>   my lord,
And mitigate
The sorrow and pain.
When you are pleased
I shall have all my heart's desires,
>   if only
You were to glance my way,
>   my lord.

'A Plea' (Pir Hasan Kabirdin)

Full of hope
I stand at your door,
O Ali!
Joining my hands,
This I ask of you:
Let me have sight of you,
O great saviour,
At your feet
                    I lay myself.

Says Pir Hasan Kabirdin,
Servant of yours:
I submit to you.
My lord,
This world is a sea
                    full of
Evil and treachery.
                    Tide,
Tide me across,
O my lord.

Notes to the Ginans

All numbers in these notes refer to the present translation. (The reader wishing to consult the Ginans in the original language, in Gujarati or Khojki sources, will find the references to these in Appendix 2).

Indication of the number of the Ginan is usually followed by a general analysis of it. Reference to specific words, lines or verses is indicated by the use of capital Roman numerals for the stanzas, and small Roman numerals for lines. Refrains, which occur after every stanza in the original and which in the English version may be repeated once or more often, are ignored in this enumeration.

As the *Saloko Nāno* is a single work, the first reference to it in these notes is to the page number (in place of the Ginan number as above).

Ginan (1). Overall, the hymn attributes all agency and power, in moving terms, to God. Minimal divine gestures, like a glance or a word, suffice to bring about a total transformation of self and world. By contrast, the self is powerless, an object acted on by divine power, rather than an acting subject. Yet, it is also a speaking, praying, poetic self. In this lies its link to the divine.

I. Note how the syntax parallels the shape of meaning. Lines i-iii, lacking a verb, are implicit statements in the original. In the translation, this 'incompleteness' is rendered by the participial form. Thus, in both, these lines sweep up towards, and come to a rest, in line iv. This, with its copula 'is' is the true statement, the climax of the stanza, requiring a full stop. The 'imperfection' of the preceding lines finds its missing complement of perfection in

186

the Lord, though it is also worth noting that it is not a closure: hope is openness.

II. The last conditional clause (v-vi) is the climax, resolving the tautology of i, and the paradox of ii-iv. Note too the dominating word (and tone-colour) 'green'. By contrast, in I, where the 'we', the praying-self, is the theme, it is the note of imperfection which predominates.

II-III. Note the Lord's transforming, transmuting attribute.

IV-V. It is worth noting the contrast between the abundance of water and the water-abstaining, would-be drinker at the shore. The decisive absence, as yet, is of the Lord's word of command. This comes forth in V. Now the lack is remedied; the thirst in the soul is quenched. Yet, the drinking is done only at the behest of the Lord's command. From self-surrender comes self-fulfilment.

Ginan (2). The structure of the poem consists of pairs of statements mentioning, or implying, opposed conditions: fire/water; companionship/aloneness; water 'here'; absence of water 'there'; shop and food 'here'; their absence 'there'. Thus, the overarching opposition of 'here' and 'there' forms the structure. The call to 'carry' the needed items links the 'here' to the 'there'. The allegorical equation of 'provision' and 'truth' frames the entire poem.

I, i. 'The five': the five cardinal vices. Common (with slight variations) in Sanskrit religious literature, they recur frequently in the Ginans. They are: desire (with a strong suggestion of sexual passion); rage or anger; greed; worldly allure or infatuation; and intoxication.

III, iv. *Vāṇiyā*: an Indian caste of merchants.

Ginan (3). The title of this Ginan, *ārti*, refers to the rite of devotional praise and celebration of the deity every evening in the temple. However, it is remarkable how, invoking Hindu doctrinal and ritual symbols, the Ginan negates them, equating the *nikalaṅki avatār* with the Persian term *shah*, i.e., (spiritual) king, and declaring the sites of Hindu devotion to be void (VI), and the 'true path' (VII) as their proper alternative.

Note too how the divine epiphany is said to be both manifest or evident (I) and elusive and hidden (V). The element of mystery, the 'abeyance of meaning', precludes (as indicated in the Introduction) a literal interpretation of the idea of divine manifestation. The divine epiphany retains a strong sense of mystery, inaccessibility, 'inscrutability'.

I, i. 'Mulberry-shaped realm': *sehtar dip*. One of the seven mythical island-continents in the cosmography to be found in the ancient Hindu treatises. Literally, it means 'the white continent'. However, in the Ginans the term becomes a pun (*sehtar* = mulberry). A mulberry shape is ascribed to the region containing Iran, where the Imam was in residence.

'Immaculate one': *nakalanki* or *nikalanki*. The Ginans' version of the *kalki*, the expected tenth *avatāra* or manifestation. Literally, 'blemishless, stain-less'. (Compare the Shia characterisation of the Imam as *ma'sum*, 'sinless').

II, ii. *Satagur Sohodev*: one of the designations of Pir Sadardin in the Ginans.

II, iii. 'Guide of twelve crores': the Ginans use the scheme of attributing to one major sage in each of the four, decreasingly virtuous ages of mythohistory, the emancipation of increasing multitudes of souls. In the first age, Pehlaj (Prahlada) is said to have delivered five crores of (50,000,000) souls; in the second age, the king Harischandra is credited with the emancipation of seven crores; in the third age, to Jujesthan (Yudhisthira) is attributed the emancipation of nine crores; in the fourth age (*kalajug*) at last, Pir Sadardin is celebrated as the saviour of twelve crores of souls. To this scheme Pir Hasan Kabirdin, Pir Sadardin's son, was later added as having surpassed the above predecessors by the emancipation of countless (infinite) crores.

Note that the above two designations of Pir Sadardin depict him in mythical, larger than life terms.

III, ii-iii. 'Unuttered utterance': a secret word for meditation.

III, iv-v. 'Eighty-four lakhs' (i.e., 8,400,000): the total number of reincarnations required, in traditional Hindu belief, for achieving final deliverance (unless the cycle is eliminated by acquisition of virtue and enlightenment in earthly life).

IV, iii. 'Seventy-one generations': the number of ancestral generations, in one Hindu tradition, believed to benefit, retroactively, from the outstanding virtuousness of a descendant.

VI, i. *Khaṭ darshan*: apparently a reference to the six schools of ancient Indian doctrine, here disqualified.

Ginan (5). The poem very likely refers to the *Kānfatā* Yogis, followers of Gorakhnāth, known for the large rings they wear in their ears after splitting the cartilage. It satirises them by pointing up the contrast between their ostentatious tokens of ascetic discipline and their inner ignorance and hollowness. The true master is the deep theme of the poem. Ignorance of him is the source of the pathetic contrast between outward show and inward emptiness described in II-VI, as is made explicit in the final, climactic stanza.

VI. 'Sixty-eight shrines': sites of Hindu pilgrimage.

VII, ii. *Jogi* = *Yogi*.

Ginan (6). A hymn of touching simplicity and rustic tenderness of tone.

I. Note the elemental simplicity of the moral principles urged here.

III. The aspiration of a humble girl to rise in society through marriage into a higher station becomes a metaphor for the desire to meet the True Master by being born into the 'right house', and set on the 'right path'. The second half of the stanza, drawing out this implication, works backward on the first half, making it a metaphor.

IV. The preceding distinction between the ordinary and elite classes is developed into an image wonderfully exact and condensed. In the narrowest of streets, two quite separate worlds come face to face: the rank and file on one side; the private, exalted dyad of master and disciple on the other. Amidst the vulgar multitudes, communication between the master and aspirant must take the form of tacit gesture, of eloquent silence, an exchange of knowing glances in which a whole, intimate world of meanings is conveyed. The original could be translated more literally as, 'like a thorn I bend'. This, however, would be an ill-fitting simile. I have therefore preferred to read the passage in terms of the conceit given here.

V, i-iv. A final summation of the foregoing contrast – a prevalence of the base, a scarcity of the precious.

'Cool': a literal translation of the original word. To be understood as 'kind' – definitely not in the American colloquial sense now in vogue.

Ginan (7). I. Four statements, in the form of short, parallel, declarative sentences. The last stands out and marks the 'point' or climax of the preceding three. But this effect is due, paradoxically, to the fact that it does *not* stand out structurally. The grammatical parallelism of the fourth statement to the preceding three mirrors the semantic parallelism. Death is just like the other events mentioned: sheer, inevitable, devastating. 'He who is born will die' is the plainest possible way of stating this crushing fact. And the plainness of the statement mirrors the starkness of the fact itself.

III. In place of the general truths stated in I, we now have four events, all of which convey dilapidation or extinction.

'Jasmine': the nearest equivalent in English to the wild flower, *kevḍo.*

III, ii-iv. 'Rope, bullocks, drawer of water:' the scene is the extraction of water from a well, in a primitive Indian village, by means of a bull.

IV. The starkness of the statements in I-III has a contrast here in images of might and opulence. But the contrast is only apparent, as the show is hollow, destined to extinction. The real essence of prosperity and power, when appearances are stripped away, is ashes. Note also the contrast in time and social relations: flourishing life, activity and power at one time, extinction at the end; aloneness at the core (vi), relatedness on the social surface.

VII. Another type of relatedness, by implication more enduring, is introduced, viz., the relation of spiritual guide (*Satagur*) and follower. In this relation, the poem declares, lie the true 'gains'.

Note how the poem's motif of life and death encompasses both nature and society (sun, flowers, water, animals on one hand, houses, irrigation, princes and palaces, family bonds on the other.) Notwithstanding Levi-Strauss, the nature-culture divide is not significant here.

A sombre, twilight air pervades the entire poem, except in the last passage, where, like rays of the setting sun finally piercing an overcast sky, the hint of a hope pierces the gathered gloom.

Ginan (8). The transformation of one's being through association with the true guide is the obvious theme. The ordinary man's impure being is sanctified much in the same way that the bitter leaves of the neem-tree come to exude the sweetness of a neighbouring sandalwood tree.

Note the range of spaces invoked – heart, wood and cosmos, and the corresponding scales of relationship, from intimate intercourse in the heart, through comradely excursion in the woods, to the companionship of thiry-three crores.

II, iv. 'Friends' (*sakhi*): literally, a woman's female friend or companion.

III. 'Thirty-three crores': a standard reference in the Ginans. Note that it coincides with the total of the proverbial numbers of emancipated souls (see note to Ginan 3, II, iii.)

Ginan (9). A hymn of tender devotion and rejoicing. It has its own complexity, however. For instance, note the contrast between the domestic and cosmic scales. Thus: the Lord's arrival at the doorstep/the epoch-long wait for his (rare) advent; personal adornment/ocean-wide liberality; personally encountered Lord/Master of earth and sky; domestic service/the way of the sun and moon. There is a seamless interplay of images of home and universe, intimacy and majesty, lowliness and almighty sovereignty.

I, vi. 'Five maids': five revered female figures of mythology or history: Anasuyā, Mātā Kuntā, Tārārāni, Draupadi, and Fātimā, the Prophet Muhammad's daughter.

III, iii. *Diwān* = Minister.

Ginan (10). It is easy, in noting the general message of this Ginan about the vanity of worldly glory, brought home by death, to miss the literary factors which turn the message into compelling poetry. What is noteworthy in this regard is how the Ginan proceeds from a given event of death – the scene of a corpse in the here and now – to a timeless, archetypal, mythological subject. The first passage is taken up by an all too individual situation of having to deal with a specific death. Taking off from this, II presents a general statement. In III, the image of a corpse gives way to that of a palace – at first glance, contrary images (the grandeur of a palace as opposed to the pathos of a dead body), yet, in reality, identical, being both made of, and returning to, dust – both valueless in the end.

The image of the palace suggests the fabulous palace of the infamous demon-king, Rāvana (Rāvan in the Ginans), and the final futility of his power, wealth and virility, which are here thrown into relief against the single, superbly powerful image of an unlit lamp causing the entire castle to be shrouded in darkness.

Against all this negativity – death, dust, hollow glory, darkness and evil – the final stanza evokes the positive, life-giving, light-granting beacons of Ali and Nabi (the Prophet).

I, iv. 'Swan': a conventional metaphor, in the Ginans, for the soul.

Rāvaṇ: The legendary ten-headed demon-king of the Ramayana, responsible for abducting Sita to his castle in Lanka, and invincible until slain by Rama in the end. The Ginan is not interested in re-telling the story, rather in using the familiar allusion, the personification of all evil, to make its moral point.

Ginan (11). V, i. Yazid: Umayyad caliph, son and successor to Mu'awiya, who ordered the murder of Husain b. 'Ali, the Imam of the Shia, and the massacre of his party at Karbala – hence the very personification, in Shia tradition, of injustice and oppression.

Ginan (12). The explicit subject is divine all-pervasiveness. The explicit design is a series of similes or comparisons, stated in declarative sentences, interspersed with imperative ones. The universe (sun, moon, etc.) as well as the human constitution are said to reflect the divine essence. Thus, the perspective is of both breadth and depth. What in the universe is a pervasiveness, becomes a *closeness* in the human context. Closeness is more than nearness. It is not merely an objective proximity, but a subjective, a felt and apprehended closeness. It is this which makes the objective fact require a subjective response. It is what links the declarative statements to the moral imperatives. What at one level is a statement of doctrine is at another level an insistence on appropriate mental outlook and action.

Note also that God is not the subject-term in the similes, rather the object of a 'simile-formation'. The listener is asked to see, consider, reckon him as 'this' in relation to 'that'. This places God outside the static terms of a simile, and emphasises Him rather as an object of human cognition and perspective.

IV, i. 'Three domains': earth, sky (heaven) and the underworld (hell).

Ginan (13). Another hymn among those which warn of the vanity of worldly glory and the inevitability of death. Yet it has a very distinctive tone, due in part to the centrality of the theme of forgetting, of the great oblivion or unconsciousness which buries the divine spark in man under clouds of illusion, and plunges him, in the hymn's startling image (given poignancy by the sombre melody of the piece) in 'pitch-black night'. This forgetfulness is not a passive absence of memory, but an active unconsciousness, which *resists* awakening. It actively fosters the illusions of the ego, of security of possessions, and of indefinite time. Awakening to time, and to the ever-present spectre of death, will bring about a transition from false to true being, personified in the true guide or master.

Ginan (14). A Ginan which combines mystical allusions, moral instruction, religious psychology and the doctrine of the guide, into a string of couplets, sung in a droning, lilting rhythm evoking a mood of sombre serenity.

I. 'Your' is meant here as a possessive adjective, not as part of a reflexive pronoun – 'your self', rather than 'yourself'. 'Your selfhood' would be a correct translation, but misleading because of its conceptual abstraction, uncharacteristic to the Ginans.

A mystical allusiveness is present here, though not the doctrine of the unity of the human soul and God to be found in full-fledged mysticism.

The moral tone (II, III, V, VII), stresses an ethical relation between man and God, as well as virtuous conduct – a point of view neglected, in favour of mystical ecstasy, in some varieties of esotericism.

II-IV. Note the idea of transformation (into 'light') through virtuous conduct in life. The experience of union with the divine is not in itself the goal; it is rather the reward of what is urged as a goal, i.e., a virtuous existence. This makes the self more a responsible agent than a beneficiary of supernatural favours. Linguistically, this seems reflected in the participle ('checking') in II, signifying the activity, as opposed to the past simple tense of verbs in III and IV, signifying the fulfilled states. (All the verbs in III and IV in the original are in the past tense, the participles in the translation being due to the exigencies of English). Likewise, the verbs in the imperative mood ('know', 'turn', 'listen', 'realise', 'follow') emphasise action, even if only mental action. This partial stress on activity (balanced by stages or states) marks the moral emphasis of the text.

V-IX. Having indicated the purification of virtuous souls and their assimilation to the divine light, the Ginan reverts to the state

A Scent of Sandalwood

preceding the enlightenment. This view of 'before' and 'after' produces the sense of the dynamic passage *from* one point *to* another. This reference to a movement, a process of transformation, leads logically to the emphasis on the divine guide in IX.

This emphasis functions as a climax. It weaves the preceding themes together. Thus, egotism and worldly passion on one hand, and ignorance of the divine guide on the other, are implicitly equated. Note too that the state of ignorance is presented as absolute, while knowledge (realisation) is qualified as an 'inward' process, this alone being genuine knowledge. In this Ginan as in some others, there is awareness of both inwardness and interiority.

X. The above themes recall the experience of enlightenment.

II, i. 'The five': see note to Ginan 2, I, i.

II, vi. *Ilallāh*: a fragment of the first article of the Muslim creed.

X, iv. 'The brow's cave': *bhamar gufā*. The inside of the forehead is regarded, in some schools of Indian contemplative philosophy, as the site of the divine epiphany.

Ginan (16). It helps to bring this Ginan to life if we imagine its scene represented in a painting. The 'pointing' terms like 'this' (I) and 'there' (VIII), help to structure the scene. The Pir, the narrator, half-turned to the spectators outside the picture, gestures towards the crowd scrambling for Ali's ark so as to escape the approaching apocalypse at the end of the final, evil age (*kaliyuga* – *kalajug* in the Ginans).

It is illuminating to note the different types of discourse present in this hymn. Firstly, the Pir *speaks to* his audience (followers). In so doing, secondly, he *describes* or *reports* the spectacle, pointing out significant components – the crowds, the ark, the figure of Ali. Thirdly, while so doing, he *expounds* and *explains*, placing the immediate scene into the framework of a wider, cosmic meaning. The typical functions of spiritual leadership – showing, describing, interpreting, and placing immediate experience in a wider frame of meaning – are present here in this vivid, at once condensed and cosmic picture (as in a miniature painting). The Pir is the central figure. For, although the figure of Ali is where all eyes would seem to be turned, it is the Pir who stands in the foreground, looking both into the picture and out at the spectators, drawing them, through this dual focus, into the action of the scene. In this way, the Pir is the mediator, *par excellence*, between the figure of Ali (Imam) and the followers. The running commentary or conversation is musically enacted in the repetition-marked rhythm of the melody. Also notable are the extremities of time, emotion and action. Adverbial phrases like 'now at last', 'at long last', 'after many a day', summon the breathless urgency of the atmosphere as Time draws to a close. The scene teems with people, rushing desperately to the last and only means of salvation, producing the busy, frenetic, desperate (yet intensely hopeful) atmosphere of final chaos and deliverance.

Ginan (18). A loose cluster of ideas, held together by the central metaphor of trade. The moral theme adds ideas of prudence, soundness, sagacity and profit. To this is added, further, the contrast between perishable and imperishable goods – an age-old metaphor with counterparts in many traditions (including the Bible and the Quran). The 'precious pearls' are the words of the spiritual guide ('the merchant' here), which demarcate right and wrong ('high and low').

Ginan (19). VI, iv. 'Vows tendered in the womb': it is a standard notion in the Ginans that the individual makes a covenant with God while still in the maternal womb, undertaking to lead a virtuous life.

Ginan (20). A delightful, charming parable, quite distinctive and individual among the Ginans. Its flowing simplicity, however, masks a complexity. It has several varying, shifting frames of discourse.

Starting with words from the proprietor to the agent (I and II), it returns to brief, anonymous words addressed to the agent in X, and to words from the proprietor (symbolising God) to the angel in XIII. In between, it is the Pir who speaks to the listener. This alternation of addressees (agent; audience of the Ginan), which is also an alternation of frames (the story within the Ginan; and its communal context) has the effect of making the listeners (audience) step into the story and identify with the figure of the agent, whose fate in the tale is humanity's fate in the world.

I-II. A scheme of time and space is established in this send-off to the agent. He is to go off, make profit and return.

III-IV. The scene shifts to the foetal beginnings of life. The polarities of dark and light, ordeal and relief, incarceration and freedom, anticipate the theme of forgetfulness, the amnesia which the Ginan considers to be the hallmark of the human condition, described from V onwards.

V-IX enumerate some major transgressions: usurpation of God's (the proprietor's) rights by man (the agent); fraud; gluttony; sensual luxury and indulgence. Underlying all these, however, is a deep-seated amnesia, spanning the promise given in V (itself an allegorical variant of the implied promise of the agent to the proprietor in I-II), and the return of memory in X. V-IX thus proceed on a different plane of consciousness from what goes before and after.

X-XII. With the summons, not only the poem's protagonist (the agent), but we, its readers or listeners, seem to be jerked into remembrance. From VI to IX, we are engrossed in the story, in the fate of the protagonist. We stand outside its frame. Now, as in III-V, we too feel addressed. The story's admonishing voice becomes our own – part of our self. It represents a moral censor, a critical self reproaching the forgetful, sleeping self. Note too how the pace changes here. In IX, the pace is relaxed, sluggish. In X, it is quickened, as if goaded by a spur. In XI there is (as it were) a sharp spurt of adrenalin, and consequently, a hurried, undignified exit from a cosy, indolent haven.

XII-XVI. In I and II, the soul (agent) was in the company of God (the proprietor), though in a passive role, receiving instructions. Then it was on its own. Now we see it in society, yet ultimately unaccompanied and alone, returning to the company of God, this time for a reckoning. It is noteworthy, though, that in XIV, unlike in I and II, no words are addressed to the agent. This divine silence marks the ultimate alienation of the soul. In fact, there is an important shift of levels in the text, from address to description, in XIII-XV (having been anticipated in XII). With this shift, we are both spectators of the scene and implicated in it, now that the distancing frame of the story has been withdrawn.

In XVI, the entire humanity becomes an addressor to God, uttering words of atonement through the Pir, who speaks on behalf of all.

The whole poem has a harmonic structure in which each plane is echoed on another, each an allegory of the other. There is no need for allegorical *interpretation*, however, not only because the allegory is obvious and transparent, but because it wholly encompasses the text, making it quite unlike texts in cultures with a literary emphasis where a hidden, philosophical message is conveyed symbolically.

Ginan (21). IV, iii. 'Twelve crores': see note to Ginan 3, II, iii.

Ginan (22). The central contrast in the poem is between the real and the fake, the authentic and inauthentic. This is crystallised in the metaphor of genuine and counterfeit money, the difference between which, as the Ginan declares, is all too obvious. Less obvious is just what the metaphor of each coin signifies. This is due to the richness of associations. One line of associations connects to mystical practice (I); another (II) to ethics (which is a recurring refrain in the original); yet another (X) extends to the moral deterioration at the end of time, and to the divine judgement to come (VII-IX). The reference to the Lord in these passages is where all the lines come together, as He is not only the truth, but the revealer of truth, the one who sifts the true from the false.

I, i. Three-streamed realm: probably a reference to the mystical symbolism (in Yoga) of the left and right nostrils, by the control of inhalations through which the adept achieves mystical experience at the third point, the bridge where the breaths come together. The terms in the Ginans for these three features are *iṅglā*, *piṅglā* and *sukhmaṇā*, all derived from Sanskrit originals prevalent in Yogic literature.

Ginan (23). This Ginan is analysed in the Interpretative Essay.

IV, ii. 'Sixty-eight shrines': see note to Ginan 5, VI.

V, iv. 'immaculate': *niraṅjan* in the original.

VII, ii. *namāz*: Muslim ritual prayer (Arabic, salat).

Ginan (25). A hymn celebrating the rite of meditation and worship in the last part of the night. The subject is enriched by a series of symbolic polarities: night/day, dark/light, dawn/last of night, sleep/wakefulness, moral pollution ('ill-gotten gains')/ purity (ablution, etc.), reality/ghostly desolation, fertility (of the night)/ghost-haunted emptiness. That the night is described as 'pregnant' is a way in which at least one of the polarities (night/day) is overcome. For, pregnancy is both life and a 'not-yet-life'. Likewise, the hymn defines dawn as 'night bearing day within her womb'. It is on the verge of delivery, but it is not daytime as yet.

197

A general emphasis is on a transformation of the soul through moral rectitude and worship, with resulting effulgence of the light (*nur*). The melodic, recurrent echo of this last term holds the whole poem together and bathes it in a mystical atmosphere. A repeated harping on the last remaining moments creates a marked effect of urgency and expectation. A particular richness of effect is present in the sudden expansion of the temporal scale, whereby the last of the night is made to stand for the last age of the world (VII). In this way, three scales of time (profane, mystical, and cosmic) are brought together. The result is a poetry whose meaning inhabits more than one level.

IV, i-ii. 'Worthiest of guests': literally, 'worthiest of mendicants'.

IV, iii. 'Unscriptable': *alakh*, the One who cannot be written (not just written *about*) i.e., who cannot be 'scripted'. This term, characterising God as beyond representation through writing, occurs often in the Ginans.

Ginan (28). III, i. 'Five thieves' (the five passions): see note to Ginan 2, I, i.

Ginan (29). Imamshah is supposed to have made a journey to Iran after the death of his father, as mentioned in the Introduction. This Ginan commemorates the invitation to proceed there by an emissary, a Chandanvir, and describes a typical journey, hazardous and resolute, in moving, romantic, yet direct and vivid (if schematic) terms.

I, i and passim. Shah: king. In the Ginans a reference to the *spiritual* king (Imam).

I, ii. *Jaṅpudip*: *Jaṅpudipva* in Sanskrit. One of the major continental 'islands' which make up the world in the mythic geography of Sanskrit religious texts. *Jaṅpudipva* includes the geographical region of India. It is in this geographical, rather than mythical sense, that the term is used in the Ginans. Here it is the Imam's message which is said to have been conveyed to *Jaṅpudip*. In most Ginans, however, the term is used in connection with the promised advent of the Imam, an event devoutly anticipated by the followers.

Ginan (30). The persistence of a primordial bond beneath the sense of a chasm separating the soul and God is remarked on in the Interpretative Essay. This bond reveals the face of God as

Love. It is what enables the Lord to be named and called on, even in the anguish of severance or separation.

What is felt as severance and absence reveals God in His other aspect, however, of wrath. Anguish at absence of the face, and the intense pining for it, recalls the power of the face as a theme in so much of world literature. (The king's complaint, in *King Lear*, of his daughter Goneril's having 'look'd black upon me' is one example; the pivotal place of the face in Levinas' philosophical works, another).

Logically, the face must already be known to be missed and pined for. For this reason, the Ginan's dominant emotion, while of acute pining and longing, is not of despair. In the very voice of yearning there is an assured presence of its object.

That it can be expressed in such confident, intimate terms is one of the hallmarks of devotional literature, and places it in a very different class from modern literature of alienation.

Ginan (31). I. Note the breathless contraction of time into ever-smaller units.

II. This effect is reinforced by another image which, likening human fragility to unbaked clay, introduces the theme of soundless, unannounced destruction.

III. Yet another image which seems to incorporate elements of each of the above. The field is progressively stripped as the deer, a marauding agent (just like time) grazes off it. Like life, the flower-crop is ever diminishing. Besides, the deer too grazes in silence.

IV. The structure of lines iii-iv offer a parallel as well as contrast to the preceding passages. All four stanzas express anxiety at the ever-contracting span of life and the imminence of divine judgement. But note how these two lines stretch out (rather than contract) as they speak of the 'reckoning of every grain'. The process of reckoning every grain is slow and drawn-out, a protracted agony. The lines take their time being articulated. In this way, the rhythm imitates – reproduces – the meaning.

V. 'Taking heed' of this shrinking span of time (and life), and the fearful reality which lies beyond, alters the emotion, replacing fear by hope. This alteration also occurs at a more subtle level: by giving voice to the hidden, mute ('soundless') dread, the poetry serves to alleviate it. Terror, when turned into speech, hence, given meaning, is reshaped into a positive emotion.

Ginan (32). Note the tone of sweet, tender, child-like intimacy. Yet this must not blind one to a certain complexity of tone and reference. The poem is not undimensional love-talk. One sign of this complexity is to be seen in the alternation of second-person address and third-person report. The lord is both spoken to and spoken of.

A related nuance is the alternation between one-to-one devotion and shared sentiment (in IV, where the 'I' of I-III is joined by 'maiden friends', in collective adoration). However, the shared (congregational) experience does not undo (or even dilute) the privileged privacy, the personal intimacy, shared between the self and the *murshid*. The appeal to fellow-devotees in IV ('maiden friends' reflects the tendency in those Ginans which speak of love for the poetic self to take on the feminine gender) is a passing one. It does not breach the walls of the sanctuary in which self and *murshid* meet in an intimate encounter (raised to a new height of lyricism in lines v-vi, and V). Note how in these passages the self is both humbled (having been blessed with the love of 'one such as this') as well as, for this very reason, privileged.

VI-VIII shift the poem to the plane of theology. This is in contrast to the foregoing passages, where there is devotion rather than theology, and no statement of doctrine.

IX returns us to the tone of deeply personal intimacy, adding to it the poignant voice of a vulnerable being who has no refuge or shelter but in the arms of the beloved other.

III, i. 'Four ages': see note to Ginan 3, II, iii.

Ginan (35). Note the characteristic opposition of external holy sites and the interior self: Ganges, Jamuna/the heart. Satagur is presented in I as a personification of all sacred sites. Yet he transcends them. He visits, while the shrines remain stationary. Further, the devotee, playing host to Satagur, is especially privileged. While the pilgrim journeys to the shrines, the Master comes to one's own home and hearth.

Though 'bathing' is not here an explicit simile, it is clearly a figure of speech. The announcement of Satagur's arrival, which is the key theme, commandeers all these images into metaphorical reference.

The image of the 'wicked' staying aloof (we might picture them haughtily standing apart) divides the populace into those who recognise the true guide and those who don't. This distinction is reiterated in II, with the additional idea that those who recognise the true guide are the elect, while the others are the vulgar masses who don't know any better. This distinction is not quite sectarian or ideological, however. For, the elect and the rank and file are not given any religious or denominational names. This permits a symbolic – hence, the broadest possible, rather than specific – interpretation. The metaphorical quality of the Ginan is by now strongly enough established to make us understand the allusion to success and failure in business in the same vein.

I, viii. Ganga and Jamna: The rivers Ganges and Yamuna.

Ginan (36). A most remarkable feature of this Ginan, apparent only on analysis, is the progress through distinct stages which it marks in the relation between self and God.

In I, the self ('maid-servant') supplicates the lord. By the end of the passage, the prayer proceeds through several lines until, in an effective climax, the desired degree of closeness to the divine presence is specified.

Reiterating this prayer, the text now names the domain where divine presence is sought – the heart. Both space and time are suggested (the latter in the reference to a 'single breath'), describing the closest possible entwinement between the self and the divine consistent with the soul's continuing speech or plea to the latter.

It is especially noteworthy how the presence of the divine *becomes an event*, rather than *being a state*. The Ginan does not report an already achieved mystical experience. It does not give us, in Wordsworth's famous words, 'emotion recollected in tranquillity'. Rather, it speaks of an experience *in process*. The words of the Ginans are a poetic rendering of the unfolding experience. The poetic self is its announcer, not its observer.

In III, the event-character reaches a climax in a statement which is, precisely, a *witnessing*. It is not to us that the words are addressed, as if in a report, but to the lord, to whom they are a direct speech. We become, as it were, privileged eavesdroppers.

In IV, there is a distantiation. Another aspect of the divine than its encompassing presence in the soul is evoked – its aspect as infinite, cosmic lord.

In V, the epic scale comes into play. 'Speaking to' gives way to 'speaking about'. Acts of divine redemption through cosmic vistas of time are recounted. But this recounting is not abstract; it is epitomised in a recall of specific, heroic, legendary figures. These names give an individual focus to an otherwise cosmic scale of space and time.

Even as we recount these cycles of acts of redemption from long ages past, we are aware of a forward movement, a sense of momentum towards an oncoming climax. This is partly realised in VI, where the scene shifts to the *future*. It is the future which is again envisioned in VII. But here, direct speech returns, and intimacy is restored. After the vastness of the divine ('boundless-ness', in IV) and of the time-scale of divine operation ('age after age', in V), we now have the divine epiphany as an intimate 'You' again.

This restored proximity comes with something of a shudder. Now that the infinity and omnipotence of God have been extolled, it comes as a poignant realisation – recalling the mystery of the divine – that He should stoop so gently, to such a delicate, tender act, as to take a weak creature's hand in His own.

The hymn ends, finally, on the same note as it began, with words of fervent supplication.

V, v-xvi. Dhruv (Sanskrit Dhruva): a legendary figure who renounced the world and was raised to heaven and granted immortality because of his devotion. Pahelāj (Sanskrit Prahlada): Faithful devotee whom Vishnu in his fourth *avatāra* rescued from his evil father. Harischandra: Legendary king who was a personification of virtue and truthfulness. He fell victim to the sage Vishvamitra who bore a grudge against him, and demanded of the king his kingdom, possessions, person and family. Destitute, the king had to do degrading work and his wife and child (Queen Tārārāṇi and Prince Rohidās) were sold as slaves to an untouch-able. All were finally redeemed through divine intervention.

Pāṇḍavas, Dropadi (Draupadi): The Pāṇḍavas are the five brothers, protagonists in the famous epic *Mahabharata*, which describes their battle with their evil hundred cousins, the Kauravas, led by the eldest brother Duryodhana. Outwitted by the Kauravas, the Pāṇḍavas suffered the humiliation of their sister Draupadi's abduction and attempted rape by Duryodhana. However, according to the legend, a fresh layer of clothing appeared, through divine aid, beneath each layer stripped off by the Kauravas, and so Draupadi stayed inviolate.

Mātā Kuntā: mother of the Pāṇḍavas and Draupadi.

For the numbers of souls saved by Pirs Sadardin and Hasan Kabirdin, see note to Ginan 3, II, iii.

VI, iv. 'Universal bride': *Vishva Kuṅvāri.* A frequently mentioned figure in the Ginans. She personifies the universe, which at the end of times is expected to wed the *nakalaṅki avatār* – an obviously mythical conception.

Ginan (39). An unusual Ginan with an enigmatic tone. Answering a question from an unidentified voice, the authorial voice proceeds to define its identity. The 'I' distinguishes itself from all kinship roles – filial, marital, maternal. All blood ties and contractual bonds are denied, and a primal tie to 'truth' is asserted.

The theme of ascetic withdrawal from home and society in this Ginan reflects an Indian ascetic (as well as a Sufi) ideal. However, the allusions here are clearly allegorical.

Ginan (41). A wonderful Ginan, remarkable for the simple, neat and graphic images in which it paints the troubles and moral disintegration to come in the last days of the world.

The disintegration is at once natural and social. Storms and famine; hate, insubordination, shameless usurpation, infidelity, incest, litigious rivalry, loss of natural feelings – in general, a 'man-eat-man' society unredeemed by any personal loyalties; irreligion and disregard for learning – all these evils go hand in hand in a remarkably seamless, comprehensive picture of final dissolution.

Note the emphasis on degree, deference, authority, hierarchy. The Ginan takes it as a given that when these are ignored or forsaken, all hell breaks loose. (Cf. Shakespeare: 'Take but degree away, untune that string,/ And hark what discord follows ... The bounded waters/Should lift their bosoms higher than the shores/ And make a sop of all this solid globe;/Strength should be lord of imbecility,/And the rude son should strike his father dead ... Then everything includes itself in power,/Power into will, will into appetite;/And appetite, an universal wolf ... Must make perforce an universal prey/And last eat up himself').

Especially worthy of note is the simultaneously topical and universal resonance of the words. The social norms upheld here are very much of one time and place. But the description feels uncannily contemporary, and could fit many periods and many places. What is it about such words, which, while expressing the norms of a particular time and place, strike universal chords?

Ginan (44). A Ginan with a folk-tale theme which (like most folk-tales) exhibits a rich complexity beneath the simplest of surfaces.

In I and the first two lines of II, we have declarative statements with verbs in the past tense, indicating a fundamental lapse of memory in the lion as well as the human soul. This forgetfulness is also a loss of identity. The lion (and by analogy, the human soul), has forfeited its regal essence, and become cowed, docile, feeble. The original state of self-awareness has been repressed, though not permanently lost.

Note too the asymmetry, so far, between the lion's loss of memory and the soul's. The lion has forgotten its leonine characteristics and mistaken himself for a lamb. But the soul, the other term in the simile, does not have such clear-cut referents. If we ask, 'what has the soul forgotten about itself?' and 'what has it now become?' we do not have clear answers. Instead, we are given a single, broad term, 'delusion'.

This linguistic feature is highly significant. The implied story of the soul's sojourn in the world has all the hallmarks of symbolic thought – non-specificity, indeterminacy, open and elastic allusiveness. This is a hallmark of all parables – discrete elements and clear outlines on the surface, generalisable meaning beneath.

II, iii-iv. Here the 'delusion' receives a precise meaning through its antonym, 'Ali'. Ali is everything that 'delusion' is not. He is reality itself. Where he is not, there is a void – precisely, delusion.

III, i-ii. These lines, repeated in refrain, form the heart of the poem. 'Ali' takes the existential verb ('is', 'will be') as 'delusion' cannot. For, delusion is an existential fake. Its content does not exist, only appears to exist. It has only an imaginery, spurious existence. Its 'is' hides an 'is not'. By contrast, Ali *is*. It is highly significant that when attached to 'Ali', 'is' (or 'will be') has no complement. We do not have sentences of the form: Ali is (or will be) X. What we have instead is only the statement that it is he who *is*.

The result is that the existential verb receives total emphasis. There is a suggestion that only Ali exists in the world of creation, all else being either derivative, or existing only in the mode of pretence.

Other linguistic elements, such as repetition of sound-units, words and syntax (with due variation of tense in the verbs), reinforce these sentences with 'Ali' for their subject. Both poetically and semantically, then, Ali is at the centre.

V-VI. New figures are added here: 'the beloved' and 'the perfect guide'. As Ali is the positive centre of gravity of the poem, we are led to identify these positive figures with him.

Conversely, we are introduced to some of the incarnations of Delusion: pride, ignorance, self-absorption.

Note too a significant shift in the tense of the narrative, from VI onwards. We are told what *will* happen, what one may look forward to, if, on the advice of the Ginan, one aligns oneself to Ali. This introduction of the future tense, and of what we are to *anticipate*, opens up the dimension of hope. The past, a story of the loss of self-knowledge, is a *fait accompli*. In contrast to this 'given', the poem now invokes a 'yet to be'. Continuing in the anticipatory mode, it reverts to the note on which the poem opened, but now with a significant change of pronouns. The lion had forgotten *himself*. Now, '*you*' – if you were to orient yourself in the way prescribed here, to Ali, will discover (or rather, rediscover) *yourself*.

In the last verse, the listener is urged to 'abide by these words'. Thus, the narrative turns into a summons. From self-knowledge (self-realisation) a commitment is born.

From the *Saloko Nāno* (Pir Sadardin)

The *Saloko Nāno* is a work of great rhythmic beauty, powerful sincerity of feeling and experience, and vivid poetic realisation. Through a series of simple images and similitudes, a central constellation of ideas is rendered into poetry. These include the primacy of truth, the indispensability of a living guide whose *raison d'être* is to lead humanity to truth, the importance of dying a true (non-physical) death, and the role of love as a passion *sui generis*, shattering all cosy, complacent ways of living in the world, putting the self in touch with what is ultimately real and ultimately good. Virtue is a central idea here. So too is a measure of interest in mystical, esoteric attainment. It will be seen, thus, that there is not only a fair number of momentous ideas here but a unitive view in which they appear as but facets of an integral vision of human destiny.

The achievement of the *Saloko* lies in conveying all this poetically. The melodic rhythm, which is like the hypnotic, repetitive advance and retreat of waves which one hears on a quiet night in a home by the beach, is a prime factor in this poetic success. Another is the continual contrasting of these ideas, realised in images, with their opposite counterparts. Thus, falsehood, ritual formalism, shrine-worship, etc., are continually exposed, in all their hollowness and futility, by being juxtaposed against opposite realities. And all this is done in simple, homely, rustic images – there is not the faintest touch of the learned, the scholastic, or the abstruse. Yet, as I try to show in these notes which follow, there is considerable complexity, which is that of an authentic vision, hence 'natural' and easy, rather than laboured and conventional.

I have found exploration of the polarities, of the kind just mentioned, a useful key to the work. Hence the attention devoted to them in the notes. But this of course is only a method, a means to an end.

Each stanza in the original is a quatrain. Each begins with the words, *Satagur kahere*, i.e., 'so says the Satagur'. 'Satagur' literally means 'true teacher' (or 'mentor', 'guide'). In a non-lyrical text, however, to translate these words every time would have been merely repetitious, rather than an aid to rhythm. I have therefore omitted them.

Pages 153–154. Note the progression in these verses, in the course of which some of the central themes which run through the work are introduced, and made to branch out. Two among these are the contrast between speech and being, and appearance and reality. Other antitheses are then added. They all twine together to carry forward the central thread of meaning.

Page 154, I, i-iv. The contrast of 'saying' with 'having' is enhanced in the original through the half-rhyming *kare* and *pāve*. These lines introduce two structurally parallel statements which assert a contrast, however, between speech and possession (saying and having).

I, v-vii. Now the 'saying' is qualified by a specification of mode: lip-service, of which the opposite mode which we expect to be inner action, a state of the heart, is not as yet specified. It will be the task of later verses to articulate the character of such inner action.

I, viii. Note the startling contrast of this line to the foregoing ones. Nothing in them has prepared us for this conclusion, the effect of which is to warn us, as later verses in the work will elaborate, that the stakes in the game of love are very high. It is indeed a matter of life and death.

II, i-ii. A note of parody is struck here – a note which will sound again, periodically, in the Ginan. The tone of I, i-iv was matter of fact; here it is ironic. Save for this difference, however, the two passages are exactly parallel, in structure as well as meaning.

III. The central theme branches out into the additional contrast between plebeian coarseness and the refined tastes of the elect.

Page 154, I. Yet another ramification: the contrast between life-destroying and light-giving properties. Present already in seed-form here is the antithesis of life and death, which provides so much of the poetic material of this Ginan.

I, i. 'Glass beads': literally, 'glass'.

I, vi. 'Poison': ingestion of powdered glass was a customary way of committing suicide in rural India.

II. The contrasting situation of those who are lucky enough to have a master to guide them and those who don't, sum up all the foregoing antitheses. This contrast works backwards on the previous ones, revealing their true purpose. Specifically, the difference between the 'junk' (dare we say, 'fast') food of the masses, and the refined fare of the gourmand, is shown up as a metaphor setting off base preoccupations with devotion to the 'name' (of God). Being thus jolted into another realm of meaning through the power of metaphor, we are the better able now to understand *all* the foregoing images as metaphors.

III. Note the simplicity of the images. It is also interesting to note the fusion of image and idea. It would be a mistake to say that the images 'illustrate' or 'symbolise' superficial devotion, devoid of love. The idea and the image are too well-blended for mere symbolisation. The idea of loveless piety, the tactile and visual sensation of plaster which will not stick (the reference seems to be to dung, used in rural settings for paving) and the sound of hollow percussion, all fuse into a single effect, which is at once idea, feeling and image.

Page 155. Another set of simple, vivid images. It is interesting to note how they vary from the image just noted above. Here there is no fusion, rather the deliberate employment of a simile to drive the underlying idea home. The image is in the service of the idea – the idea being the redeeming power of the True Master, and the destruction awaiting those who follow pretenders to that role. The idea is prior to the image – it *suggests* the image, which in I is sketched in all its vivid, comic simplicity, and then in II, generalised into a broad lesson. Passage III steers the image into an allegorical statement, completed in the next stanza, which supplies a spiritual equivalent for each of the items in the concrete image. Despite this 'spiritualisation', however ('God's name', 'weight of truth', 'wind of love'), the concrete, material images are retained. It is these which give poetic body to the ideas.

Page 156. The theme of salvation is now linked to that of love implied in the 'We' (the Shah and the Pir), bearers of salvation, worthy of the devotees' love. The gift of salvation is contrasted with the superficial glamour of wealth and status, as well as the hollow rites and austerities of Hindu sectaries who, in ignorance of the True Guide, fail to attain immortality. Note the passing reference to the 'light divine' in II, ix. The image of light will be a rich source of ideas in succeeding verses. For now, note how ignorance of light is equated with ritualism, and hence, by association, with the 'lip-service' devalued at the outset.

Page 157. The long road to human birth, and the value of human life, are recalled in juxtaposition to images of 'half-hatched' life, blindness and the ever-present shadow of death. Cancelling these privations is the supreme positive: 'the high risen sun'. Note the idea of necessary mutilation (in the image of the ruby requiring to be pierced before being threaded). Though at first glance a new idea, it was already anticipated in the 'dealing in heads' mentioned in p.153, I, viii. The image blends into the idea that love is an ordeal, requiring sacrifice – one of the central ideas running through the work.

I, i. 'Four mines': a traditional categorisation of life according to their (four different) modes of origination.

Page 158. The glory of the risen sun, its light-shedding, life-giving power is one of the central images in the *Saloko*. It is explicitly identified, moreover, with the Satagur (True Teacher or Guide) in all the four verses translated here.

Page 159. The transformation of base substance into gold through alchemy is one of the familiar metaphors in the Ginans for the transformation of the human self, through moral purification, into a part of the divine. It has an intrinsic affinity, furthermore, with the notion of the ordeal, the 'fiery test' to which the soul has to submit to be cleansed of its moral impurities.

Also worth noting is the process whereby the larvae, unlike the fully-fledged insect, *comes to be* the wasp. On pp.153–154, difference was the dominant note. Now we observe that there is a potential identity in difference. Taking this to its logical extreme, we might say that there is no polarity which is ultimately irresolvable, nothing which is ultimately irredeemable. (But this is only a logical potentiality in the Ginan's scheme, which also acknowledges the opposite idea – irrevocable damnation.)

I, v. 'Philosopher's stone': *Pāras* in the original. A mythical substance believed to transmute base metal into gold.

Page 160. The metaphorical exploration of death (with the implicit, underlying question, 'what does death really mean?') is a significant intellectual contribution of this Ginan. (By 'intellectual' what is meant here is the development of an idea – not, of course, the philosophical, logical or argumentative exposition of a thesis, a system of ideas).

What the *Saloko* says in this regard, in a nutshell, is that there is death, and there is death. The different meanings of death are established, first, by modality – a true manner, as opposed to a false manner, of dying. This, however, begs the question: what, precisely, is the difference? The answer is found through transitive consideration: what does one die *to*, and die *into*? The answer here is that one dies to the world, or to the passions ('world' and 'passion' are equated as, according to the Ginans, it is in the nature of the passions to bind the self to external objects).

What one dies into is left at 'wisdom divine', though other verses will extend the definition. But the commanding figure into whom, and through whom, one dies, having died to the 'world', is the True Guide – who, paradoxically, is the epitome of life, and a giver of the life of the spirit.

Note how, by invoking the vast cycle of births, and observing that in all this time, the lower passions remain unconquered, the Ginan emphasises their formidable power.

II, v. 'Eighty-four', i.e., eighty-four lakhs. See note to Ginan 3, III, iv-v.

III, i. 'Five furies': see note to Ginan 2, I, i.

Page 161. First, a conventional Indian belief about the sacred origin of the Ganges is repeated without comment, although in the reference to streams from the land running into it, there is already a tacit and ambiguous hint of a profane, polluted flow.

In the next passage, the Ganges as a sacred concept is undone. The river is desacralised, and the shrines near it, conceptually demolished. First (lines i-ii), there is a neutral, non-judgemental mention of the Ganges as a site for shrines. Then (lines iii-iv), the Satagur is proclaimed as the shrine. But if he is to be defined as a 'shrine', the meaning of 'shrine' must alter radically. Once a living person is defined as a 'shrine', the word can no longer apply to structures – which by definition are 'dead'. They are thus re-defined as profane, 'dead' things, unworthy of homage. It is interesting to compare this rhetorical operation with the Biblical and Quranic re-definition, and denunciation, of idols.

In a final stroke, the Satagur expressly dissociates himself from the Ganges, making its supposed sacredness evaporate into a figment.

Page 162. These passages continue the note introduced above, varying it with the opposition between the desolation of the wilderness, and the society of communal dwelling. What mediates this opposition is the central figure of the 'living person' (the True Guide) who points the way from the deadly jungle to the living amenity of the town, and who gives direction to the lost soul. (The soul in *perdition*, the Latin etymology of which term, still alive in the Romance languages, perfectly captures the semantic connection between the ideas of loss and damnation).

IV, v-viii. These lines are striking, and we must ask why. The image is just because it completes the foregoing image of the void with the suggestion of sterility, fruitlessness. But it is also poetically arresting, being a dramatic evocation of the non-drama of its subject.

Page 163. This highly effective passage has been commented on in the Interpretative Essay. The effect lies in its rendering of a familiar fact, staring one in the face, yet scarcely noticed, into an enigma, and so into a theme of urgent (and deeply productive) meditation.

Page 164. I continues the theme of the verses on pp.161–162.

II. Having been discredited in its normal meaning as an objective place or structure, the 'shrine', now with an altered, metaphorical meaning, is located in the heart.

Page 165. Here we have a reference to meditative technique. This is the explicit topic of I as well as III, which also evokes the intimacy and privacy of conversational exchange between the worshipper and his God, which constitutes meditation. The practice of meditation is grounded, in Indian thought, in a sacred anatomy, physiology and psychology, alluded to here.

II and III verbalise, poetically, what is essentially impossible to verbalise. This is done through the image of the wave dipping back into the ocean. Unity defies verbalisation, as to put it into words is to undo the unity. The only device available to a poet, then, is to describe not unity, but the process of unification. This calls for the specific poetic skill of finding a fitting and economical image, free from other, distracting, overtones, which will convey the process, and *only* the process, rightly and adequately.

III, i. *Zikr* (Ar. *dhikr*): a term which literally means 'remembrance', but has the special meaning, in Sufi orders, of a recitation of the divine name in a state of collective ecstasy or trance. *Zikr* in the Ginans has a different (though not unrelated) meaning. While referring to meditative absorption in the divine name, it indicates an individual, *interior* process (a sense also present in Sufi traditions, but one which should be distinguished from the better known collective practice).

Page 166. This passage recapitulates the motifs of truth and love (and the beloved), all sounded at various points in the work. The present verse adds the new domain of physical being and ornamentation. Note too the re-appearance of the idea of transformation (cf. p.159, I-III).

Page 167. I. The images of the sun, the morning light which banishes darkness, and the opposite image of blindness, have been developed already in foregoing verses (cf. pp.156, II; 157, III-IV; 158, I-IV). Here, sunlight is said to be found in the heart, thus carrying forward the metaphoric meaning of 'light' (cf. pp.164, II and 165, I). Note, additionally, the allusion to 'every heart', which, in its suggestion of universality, parallels the all-pervasive reach of the sun.

II. Cf. pp.153, I-II; 154, III; 156, I and 162, I, for statements of the futility of all religious worship lacking in love; p.157, II for the worthlessness of a being untouched by passion (the ruby and the lotus are two distinct, incarnate images of a single theme); and p.165, II-III for the converse theme of inter-penetration.

II, vii. 'skin': *ang* in the original, which is better translated as 'being'. I have rejected this, however, as its disyllabic and other phonetic features interfere with the rhythm.

III recapitulates the argument of pp.153, I-II and 154, III. IV adds, to this recapitulation, two other clusters of ideas developed earlier: the disjunction between lips and heart, which also picks up, at the level of deeper logic, the unpierced ruby and the waterproof lotus; and the complex of ideas expounded in the image of the boat-trip, p.155, I-IV.

Page 168. On the surface, a new idea is introduced: self-important, pedantic learning, hollow at the core. But in reality there is no break, rather a new development, a new ramification, of themes such as those developed in p.156, I-III and even p.164, I, not to mention the more subtle echoes of passages which interchange life with death – seeing in 'true' death the consummation of life, and conversely here, a kind of death (ignorance and perdition) in pointless activity ('running around'), book-knowledge, ostentation and crowd adulation.

Also noteworthy is the element of farce, burlesque, caricature.

Page 169. See my comments on this marvellous passage in the Interpretative Essay. The power of these lines springs from the way in which a sophisticated idea is fused with an utterly simple, perfectly homely image.

Page 170. These lines name several forms of injury or privation (poisoning, thirst, hunger) and balance them with an identification of their cures (antidote, drink, food). But the commanding idea is the moral or spiritual pathology of 'pollution', and the curative virtue of God's name. When we reach this explanation (lines viii-ix), our reading of the preceding lines is re-adjusted, in a realisation of their role as similitudes.

Page 171. I. Note the exact contrast of this image to the one in p. 157.

II. The idea that the value of a pearl can alter both ways, that it can decrease and increase, is a poetic echo to the theological idea that human nature is poised between two possibilities: elevation to divinity, and degradation to bestiality. This view of human dualism is implicit in the Ginans.

II. The theme of inversion of values (for truthfulness in the Ginans' view equals harmony with the natural order of things) is a central thread in their conception of moral evil.

III. The moral chasm which divides adherents of truth from their opposite number is an idea linked to another notion frequently expressed in this and other Ginans – namely, that the former are a tiny minority, a spiritual aristocracy, in comparison with the vast majority who live in and by falsehood.

II, viii-x. Literally, 'will declare seven to be five'. This is only the most obvious instance in the business of translation where the idiom of one language requires to be rendered into the *idiom* (rather than the equivalent *words*) of another.

Page 173. I. An arresting passage. Part of its dramatic effect lies in the direct speech; part in its vigorous, colloquial, unsparing, indeed brutal, tone; and part again, in the shock of the repudiation of a terrible death, courted in the service of a sacred ideal, as fundamentally misguided. It is said here to be untrue to the very ideal, i.e., love and faithfulness (to the deceased), in whose name the widow immolates herself. Convention deceives, even to the point of making people court a dreadful martyrdom in the cause of ideals which are belied rather than served in the act. The underlying question, obviously, is about the nature of death, raised before (p.160, I-III). The institution of *sati* was condemned by Indian reformist thinkers in recent history on modern, humanitarian grounds. It is interesting to note the difference in this medieval dismissal of it on mystical grounds. It will be seen that like the otherwise very different humanitarian critiques, it carries a stronger rational force than attacks on merely ideological (i.e., 'Islamic' vs. 'Hindu') grounds. At the same time, we might also note the limitation of a purely mystical critique such as this, due to the absence in it of *social* criticism. The social vision came into its own only with the advent of modernity, the tradition of liberal politics and the outlook of modern sociology.

II. Another enchanting passage. Its power lies in the way in which several sophisticated ideas have been so well 'metabolised' – so perfectly realised as convictions – that they no longer demand effort of expression, but are stated with natural confidence, brevity and simplicity. These qualities reflect a mature development, rather than an early state, of a culture. The clarity, the terse and straightforward quality of such language, seems effortless because the mind is not struggling with (not self-consciously aware of) a complex idea. The complexity has become subsumed, rather, in an assured conviction of the truth of the principles which are put forward.

The idea that true death is the destruction of the ego, engrossed in worldly vanities, is already the product of a mature vision, which has not only developed the appropriate conceptions of 'world' and 'self', but has also worked out the relations between them. This element of maturity, of complex sensibility, will become clearer upon the following consideration. Death is by definition the farthest extreme of passivity. The note of passivity is reiterated here in the words, 'made themselves low as the earth'. The succeeding image of puppets both repeats and modulates this theme of self-effacement. Puppets have no will of their own; they are the plaything of another will. Here, the other operative will is of God, which is also the will present at the core of human life. What from one point of view appears to be death, is from another angle, life abundant. This paradox is tacitly present in the notion that these puppets (human beings who have overcome them-selves) possess speech; and that what they utter is the Supreme Word, the fount of all life. Thus, true death (defined in these terms) turns out to be identical with true life.

I, ii. *Sati* (Anglicised spelling: suttee): a widow who, acting according to an ancient Hindu custom, now banned, chooses to immolate herself by joining the corpse of her husband on the funeral pyre as a sign of devotion to him.

II, vii. 'Puppets': literally, statues. But 'statue' has connotations of size, monumentality, which is certainly not implied here. 'Statuettes' or 'figurines' convey the implied dimensions more accurately, but I have rejected these alternatives because of their unsatisfactory effect on the rhythm. Moreover, a puppet acts, albeit upon being manipulated. This idea is implicit in the original, but not in the foregoing English terms.

II, viii. 'Five organs': five senses.

Page 174. I. The beauty of this passage lies in its evidence of a mature vision fresh enough to perceive very simple facts, and to see them, at the same time, in the light of a refined wisdom. It is the simultaneous, unified operation of *both* faculties which produces a verse such as this. It is a truism that the rich are few in relation to the poor, especially in societies lacking the comparatively recent phenomenon of 'middle classes' (where 'rich' and 'poor' have ambiguous and shifting meanings). What we have here is the working of a mind which, while observing this fact, is also conscious of an elasticity in the very meaning of 'rich' and 'poor'. The perceptual and metaphorical sensibilities work together, so that while the words 'rich' and 'poor' stay constant, the idea of their numerical disproportion is turned into the relation of a *qualitatively* different minority and majority (the fortunate few who enjoy the gift of love, and a vast majority leading loveless lives).

II. Another memorable passage. Two parallel negative statements (exactly parallel, in structure, in the original) dissociate love from the external world. The third statement locates it in the heart, thus joining up with the central antitheses of heart/stone, life/death, love/absence of love, etc., which run through the entire work. Emphasis on the heart is now combined with the additional suggestion of spontaneous generation, thus introducing a fresh contrast between spontaneity and contrivance (in the form of farming and trade).

The last declaration comes as a shocking climax – the tonic of love turns out to be fatal; it consumes and destroys the very womb, as it were, which gives it birth. But this self-destruction is a supreme joy. What we have here is a religious version of the familiar idea of love as a source of sweet torment.

Note too the suggestion of sublime helplessness – the heart or soul as a plaything of the divine beloved. In the deep structure of the poetry, this verse links up with p.173, II.

Page 175. These verses resume the play on various meanings of death, the wounding impact of the divine encounter (cf., e.g. p.157, II; 174, II), and return to the image of rock or stone (cf. p.164, I), to exploit its poetic possibilities. The result is an enhanced vividness of that image due to the poetic realisation of the texture – the impregnable hardness – of rock. Further, this idea of hearts hard as stone is now firmly linked to the theme of absence of the True Guide.

Page 176. These passages exert a haunting effect which runs parallel to the theme of love's stabbing, wounding, slaying power. There is a rare dramatisation here because the images are taken from the battlefield and from the gallows. These are settings for spectacles of torture, death and heroic self-sacrifice. The Ginan lifts the images off these theatres and transfers them to the domain of the heart. Goings-on in the interior domain take on the shape and colour, the dramatic momentum, of events usual to the former context. The fusion of these domains determines not just the expressive style, but the very conception of love between the self and the divine beloved. No doubt, Ginanic poetry lacks the kind of richness we enjoy in poetry which takes the *external* world as its object. But this limitation is compensated for by the richness of characterisation of *interior* states and modes.

Note again the sophisticated conception of love, *embedded* rather than consciously formulated in these passages, as an at once life-taking and life-giving experience.

Page 177. I. The Lord is here re-affirmed, more explicitly than before, as the supreme value through which everything precious in life derives its worth. The idea of barter or trade recalls passages like p.153, I; while the contrast between the spiritual aristocracy and 'common folk' (asserted in pp.156, I; 157, II; 168; 171, I and 175, II) is now recapitulated in the terse symbolism of price and pricelessness.

II, III. The timeless, general principles stated so far now give way to an awareness of time. And with this, a wedge is driven between the past and the present, the bygone and the current, yesterday and today, then and now. Passage II was utilised in modern Indian Ismaili preaching – mainly through the first half of the last century – to support the doctrine of the supremacy of the current Imam, and of his current decrees, over all preceding ones.

Note how the image of the sun is now adapted to this consciousness of time. In passages such as pp. 157, IV, 158, I-II and p. 167, I, the present time, the instant at hand, was implicit in the idea of the 'risen sun'. This, however, was a *generalised present*. Now, the appearance of the sun is visualised in a *specific present*. Temporal specificity thus moves into the foreground in these verses, marking a contrast between the present and the past.

III, viii and IV, i. 'Formula': literally, 'elixir'.

216

Pages 178–179. As the long procession of verses, with their rising and falling rhythm, their surging energies and cadences, the successive themes rising to the fore, modulating, subsiding into the background, and re-emerging in combination with other themes – as all this draws to an end, the time-scale and spatial frame of the Ginan spreads out to take in cosmic vistas. True to the scheme of the past being superseded by the present, the virtuous accomplishments of legendary figures are invoked strictly in a progressive gradient leading to the crowning phase of the new faith, *satpanth*, represented in Pir Sadardin's achievement, itself mythologised, here as elsewhere in the Ginans. There is a certain grandeur in the concluding climax of this long work, in which a succession of simple, rural images and metaphors introduce and elaborate a moral, mystical vision of human existence.

'A Plea' (Pir Hasan Kabirdin)

Although subsumed, in the original texts, in miscellaneous collections (without any distinguishing indication), this hymn has been singled out here as an example of the consistent tone of ardent supplication which is such an impressive quality of Ginans in this genre. The Interpretative Essay in this volume remarks on the sheer, elemental clarity of its moral vision and the submergence of individual consciousness in a collective voice in its choral recitation.

Appendix 1: Note on Transliteration

Concerned to avoid technicalities, I have kept transliterations from the original to a minimum, bowing only to necessity.

The Gujarati script has a standard scheme for Romanised transliteration (easily adaptable to Khojki), used by the Library of Congress and the British Library. I have used this as a guide, making small departures when these are likely to be more readily recognisable to a general reader with no linguistic specialisation. Thus, I have substituted the more obvious *ch* for the standard *c* (necessitating the next consonant in the Gujarati alphabet to be rendered as *chh*). Likewise, I have substituted *sh* for *ś*, and have ignored the distinction between *i* and *ī* and *u* and *ū*.

For uninitiated readers, the following general clues may be useful. Gujarati consonants have an inherent vowel. Thus, a strict transliteration will register *ka* rather than *k*. An English-speaking reader unfamiliar with Gujarati must thus avoid the mistake of reading the vowels in *Satagur* represented by *a*, as the *a* in 'man', or *a* in 'father'. Indeed, the second *a* in *Satagur* may safely be ignored in pronunciation, except as a reminder that the preceding consonant is to be fully pronounced rather than elided. In words which have become entrenched in usage, however, I have retained the customary spelling – thus, *Satpanth* rather than *Satapanth*.

The inherent '*a*' at the end of Sanskrit words is neither written nor pronounced in Gujarati. This has led in the present work to two distinct transliterations of certain words, e.g. *avatāra* and *avatār*, according as to whether the intended reference is to the term in Sanskrit, or in the Ginans, respectively. However, in the transliteration of first lines (in Appendix 2), a final '*a*' has been inserted in words which, when sung as part of the line, necessitate utterance of this vowel. This should ensure correspondence, on this point, between the transliteration here and the lines as they are heard in oral performance.

A commonly occurring notation is *ṅ*. This represents nasalisation (e.g. of the *a* in *Jaṅpudip*).

As a general rule, in the transcription of sounds from Indian languages, a dot under a consonant indicates its retroflex counterpart (produced, that is, with the tongue curling towards the back of the roof of the mouth).

No diacritical marks have been used in Arabic or Persian words, which at any rate occur only in my historical analysis (chiefly the Introduction), and not in the Ginans themselves (where words of Arabic *derivation* ought to be treated as Indicized rather than foreign).

I have made an exception, however, by retaining the spelling, 'Muhammad' when it refers to the Prophet, as it is so well-established as to make the Ginanic form, 'Mahmad', seem idiosyncratic.

In keeping with the philosophical distinction I have urged in the Introduction between a given figure in a religious text and the historical figure from which it takes its name, a name like 'Ali b. Abu Talib refers in this form to the historical figure (quoted in my historical analysis) while the Indicized spelling, transcribed as Ali (i.e., without the sign for the Arabic '*ayn*) refers to the figure as he appears (or better, the figure who appears) in the Ginans.

In well-known words like 'Quran', 'Imam' or, for that matter, 'Ismailism', the signs for the distinctive Arabic consonants have been omitted altogether.

Similarly diacritical marks have been omitted from relatively well-known words (e.g. *Shah*).

Words from Gujarati have been supplied with diacritical marks (with modifications as indicated above), principally as it is the main language of the literature which is the subject of this work. However, diacritical marks have been omitted in many proper nouns, such as the names of the Pirs (which, moreover, have for the most part, been transcribed in line with established usage) as well as in place-names.

Appendix 2: Sources and Index of First Lines

The following procedure for referring to the Ginans has been used in this Appendix. The opening (first) line of each Ginan is given in transliteration. This is followed (in parenthesis) by Roman numerals indicating the stanzas from the original which have been translated. The reader should bear in mind that, often enough, selected verses have been translated, and not the entire Ginan. A hyphen here denotes inclusive sequence (e.g. I-X) while an '&' (e.g. I & II) indicates that the respective stanzas have been merged (for poetic or formal reasons) into a single passage in English. The reader is reminded again that for reasons discussed in the section on translation in the Introduction, the length of the passages in English may not correspond to the length of the passages in the original.

Beneath this notation, is the reference to the Khojki edition, along with the number of the Ginan and/or the page. This is followed by the reference to the Gujarati edition, followed again by the number of the Ginan and/or the page. References to the Khojki and Gujarati editions are given in abbreviated form (see the select bibliography for the complete reference).

For the *Saloko Nāno* (see the bibliography for the complete reference) the Roman numerals refer to the numbers of the quatrains in the original.

Index of First Lines
Miscellaneous Ginans

21. *Satanā sarovara sarāsara bhariyā* (I, II, VII)
    Part Four, 43, pp. 70–71; *Pir Sadardin,* 33, pp. 32–33.
22. *Traveṇi saṅsār māṅhe zilaṅtā* (I-VIII)
    Part Four, 68, pp. 127–128; *Pir Sadardin,* 44, pp. 51–52.
23. *Hamadil khālak Allāh sohi vaseji* (I-XI)
    Part Four, 46, pp. 101–102; *Pir Shams,* 36, pp. 40–41.
24. *Hathi hathi parbata toleṅde baṅde* (I-III)
    Part Five, 53, pp. 93–94; *Pir Shams,* 48, p. 54.
25. *Nur veḍa nur piyo* (I-V)
    Part One, 67, pp. 116–117; *Pir Sadardin,* 90, pp. 91–92.
26. *Kutuṅba parivār sajnā* (I, II)
    Part Six, 19, p. 19; *Pir Hasan Kabirdin,* 74, p. 105.
27. *Hardama karo abhiāsa* (I, II & III, IV, VI, VIII, IX)
    Part Four, 101, p. 193; *Saiyad Imāmshāh,* pp. 253–254.
28. *Marnā hayre jarura* (I, II, IV, V, VII, VIII)
    Part Four, 97, pp. 188–189; *Saiyad Imāmshāh,* pp. 250–251.
29. *Shāhnā khaṭa āyā virā jaṅpudipa maṅhe* (I-IX, X & XI, XIII)
    Part Five, 54, pp. 94–95; *Saiyad Imāmshāh,* 99, pp. 131–132.
30. *Uṅchāre koṭa bahu vechnā* (I-IV)
    Part One, 2, p. 5; *Pir Hasan Kabirdin,* 2, p. 3.
31. *Saiyāṅji more ḍāra lāgo* (I-IV)
    Part Five, 34, p. 63; *Saiyad Imāmshāh,* p. 255.
32. *Sāhebaji tuṅ more mana bhāve* (I-VIII)
    Part Five, 37, pp. 67–68; *Saiyad Imāmshāh,* p. 218.
33. *Miṭhḍuṅ āṅhi bolo* (I-IX)
    Part One, 86, pp. 149–150; *Pir Shams,* 5, pp. 3–4.
34. *Kamalne fule prāṇi bāvā bhamere bhamarlo* (I, I, III-V)
    Part Two, 81, pp. 161–162; *Pir Sadardin,* 124, p. 128.
35. *Satagura padhāriyā tame jāgajo* (I, II, IV)
    Part Three, 83, pp. 161–162; *Pir Hasan Kabirdin,* pp. 121–122.
36. *Darashana dio morā nātha* (I & II, III-VI, VI & VII & VIII & IX & X & XI, XIII, XIV)
    Part Four, 98, pp. 189–191; *Saiyad Imāmshāh,* pp. 251–252.
37. *Avichala Allāh avichala khālak* (I, II, V, VII)
    Pir Sadardin, 105, pp. 110–111.
38. *Praṇiḍo chhe mātino* (I, III, V-VII)
    Part One, 99, pp. 175–176; *Pir Sadardin,* 97, pp. 97–98.
39. *Eka shabada suṇo mere bhāi* (I-III, IV & V, VIII-XI)
    Part Three, 84, pp. 162–163; *Pir Shams,* 33, p. 37.
40. *Aba teri mahobata lāgi* (I-IV, VI, VII, IX, X)
    Part Two, 84, p. 165; *Pir Shams,* 24, p.23.
41. *Pāḷa fāṭine nira ulaṭayā* (I, I, II, IV-VIII, X-XIII, XV-XVII, XXII-XXV)
    Part Three, 56, pp. 110–114; *Pir Sadardin,* 151, pp. 158–161.

42. *Sakhi māri ātamanā udhār ke alagā ma jājore* (I-V)
    Part Three, 31, p. 53; *Pir Sadardin*, 137, p. 141.
43. *Satagura srevo tame madharāte jāgo* (I-IV, V & VI)
    Part One, 72, p. 122; *Pir Sadardin*, 95, p. 96.
44. *Kesari siṅha sarupa bhulāyo* (I-V)
    Part Six, 31, pp. 35–36; *Pir Shams*, 59, pp. 63–64.

Saloko Nāno

'A Plea' (Pir Hasan Kabirdin)

Āsha tamāri sri ho kāyama sāmi (I-IX)
Part Four, 49, pp. 87–88; *Pir Hasan Kabirdin*, 43, pp. 68–69.

Appendix 3: Select Bibliography

The following is a list of original sources drawn upon for translations in this volume, and of selected works of secondary scholarship. Not all the works cited in the Introduction are included here, the aim being only to indicate works with a specific and substantial focus on the Ginans.

A. Editions

Khojki

100 Ginānni Chopaḍi: Bhāg Pahelo. Bombay, undated. [cited as *Part One*]
100 Ginānni Chopaḍi: Bhāg Bijo. Bombay, 1926. [cited as *Part Two*]
100 Ginānni Chopaḍi: Bhāg Trijo. Bombay, 1926. [cited as *Part Three*]
100 Ginānni Chopaḍi: Bhāg Chotho. Bombay, undated. [cited as *Part Four*]
100 Ginānni Chopaḍi: Bhāg Pāṅchamo. Bombay, 1934. [cited as *Part Five*]
100 Ginānni Chopaḍi: Bhāg Chhaṭho. Bombay, 1933. [cited as *Part Six*]
Saloko Moto tathā Nāno, Bombay, 1934.

Gujarati

Mahān Ismāili Saṅt Pir Sadardin Rachit Ginānono Saṅgrah 1. Bombay, 1952. [cited as *Pir Sadardin*]
Mahān Ismāili Saṅt Pir Shams Rachit Ginānono Saṅgrah 2. Bombay, 1952. [cited as *Pir Shams*]
Mahān Ismāili Saṅt Pir Hasan Kabirdin ane Bijā Sattādhāri Piro Rachit Ginānono Saṅgrah 3. Bombay, undated. [cited as *Pir Hasan Kabirdin*]
Mahān Ismāili Dharmaprachārak Saiyad Imāmshāh ane Bijā Dharmaprachārak Saiyado Rachit Ginānono Saṅgrah 4. Bombay, 1954. [cited as *Saiyad Imāmshāh*]

B. Translations and Secondary Sources

Allana, G (ed. and trans.).
Ginans of Ismaili Pirs Rendered into English Verse. Karachi, 1984.

Asani, Ali S.
'Ginān', in *Encyclopaedia of Religion*, vol. 5, ed. M. Eliade. New York, 1987, pp. 560–561.
'The Khojkī Script: A Legacy of Ismāʿīlī Islam in the Indo-Pakistan Subcontinent', *Journal of the American Oriental Society*, 107, 3 (1987), pp. 439–449.
'The Khojahs of Indo-Pakistan: The Quest for an Islamic Identity', *Journal of the Institute of Muslim Minority Affairs*, 8, 1 (1987), pp. 31–41.
The Bujh Niranjan: An Ismaili Mystical Poem. Cambridge, Mass., 1991.
'The Ginān Literature of the Ismailis of Indo-Pakistan: Its Origins, Characteristics and Themes', in *Devotion Divine: Bhakti Traditions from the Regions of India*, ed. D. Eck and F. Mallison. Groningen-Paris, 1991, pp. 1–18.
The Harvard Collection of Ismaili Literature in Indic Languages: A Descriptive Catalog and Finding Aid. Boston, 1992.
'The Ismaili *Gināns* as Devotional Literature', in *Devotional Literature in South Asia: Current Research, 1985–8*, ed. R. S. McGregor. Cambridge, 1992, pp. 101–112.
'Bridal Symbolism in Ismāʿīlī Mystical Literature of Indo-Pakistan', in *Mystics of the Book: Themes, Topics, and Typologies*, ed. R. A. Herrera. New York, 1993, pp.389–404.
'The Ismaʿili *Gināns*: Reflections on Authority and Authorship', in *Mediaeval Ismaʿili History and Thought*, ed. Farhad Daftary. Cambridge, 1996, pp. 265–280.

Chunara, A. J.
Nuram Mobin. 4th ed. Bombay, 1961

Hooda, V. N (trans.).
'Some Specimens of Satpanth Literature', in *Collectanea*: Vol. 1, ed. W. Ivanow. Leiden, 1948, pp. 55–137.

Ivanow, W.
'The Sect of Imam Shah in Gujrat', *Journal of the Bombay Branch of the Royal Asiatic Society*, New Series 12 (1936), pp. 19–70.
'Satpanth', in *Collectanea*: Vol. 1, ed. W. Ivanow. Leiden, 1948, pp. 1–54.

Kassam, Tazim R.
Songs of Wisdom and Circles of Dance: Hymns of the Satpanth Ismāʿīlī Muslim Saint, Pīr Shams. Albany, New York, 1995.

Khakee, Gulshan.
The Dasa Avatāra of the Satpanthi Ismailis and Imam Shahis of Indo-Pakistan. Ph.D thesis. Harvard University, 1972.

Khan, Dominique-Sila.
'The Coming of Nikalank Avatar: A Messianic Theme in Some Sectarian Traditions of North-Western India', *Journal of Indian Philosophy,* 25 (1997), pp. 401–426.

and Zawahir Moir.
'Coexistence and Communalism: The Shrine of Pirana in Gujarat', *South Asia, Journal of South Asian Studies,* XXII (1999), pp. 133–154.
'The Lord will Marry the Virgin Earth: Songs of the Time to Come', *Journal of Indian Philosophy,* 28 (2000), pp. 99–115.

Mallison, Françoise.
'Les Chants Garabī de Pir Shams', in *Litteratures Medievales de l'Inde du Nord,* ed. F. Mallison. Paris, 1991, pp. 115–138.
'Muslim Devotional Literature in Gujarati: Islam and Bhakti', in *Devotional Literature in South Asia: Current Research, 1985–1988,* ed. R. S. McGregor. Cambridge, 1992, pp. 89–100.

and Zawahir Moir.
'"Recontrer l'Absolu, O Ami..": Un Hymne Commun aux Hindous Tantriques et Aux Musulmans Ismaeliens du Saurashtra (Gujarat)', *Puruṣārtha,* 19 (1996), pp. 265–176.

Moir, Zawahir.
'Bībī Imām Begam and the End of the Ismaili Ginānic Tradition', in *Studies in Early Modern Indo-Aryan Languages, Literature and Culture: Research Papers, 1992–1994, Presented at the Sixth Conference on Devotional Literature in New Indo-Aryan Languages, Held at Seattle, University of Washington, 7–9 July 1994,* ed. Alan W. Entwistle and Carol Salomon. New Delhi, 1999, pp. 249–265.

'The Life and Legends of Pir Shams as Reflected in the Ismaili Ginans: A Critical Review', in *Constructions Hagiographiques dans le Monde Indien: Entre Mythe et Histoire,* ed. Françoise Mallison. Paris, 2001, pp. 365–384.

Nanji, Azim.
The Nizārī Ismāʿīlī Tradition in the Indo-Pakistan Subcontinent. Delmar, NY, 1978.

Poonawala, I.
'Nūr Satgur', in *The Encyclopaedia of Islam, New Edition, Vol. VIII,* ed. C. E. Bosworth et. al. Leiden, 1995, pp. 125–126.
'Pīr Ṣadr al-Dīn', in *The Encyclopaedia of Islam, New Edition, Vol. VIII,* ed. C. E. Bosworth et. al. Leiden, 1995, p. 307.

Appendix 3: Select Bibliography

'Pīr Shams', in *The Encyclopaedia of Islam, New Edition, Vol. VIII*, ed. C. E. Bosworth et. al. Leiden, 1995, p. 307.

Shackle, Christopher and Zawahir Moir.
Ismaili Hymns from South Asia: An Introduction to the Ginans. Richmond, Surrey, 2000.

Virani, Shafique.
The Voice of Truth: Life and Works of Sayyid Nūr Muḥammad Shāh, a 15th/16th Century Ismāʿīlī Mystic. M.A. thesis. McGill University, 1995.